D0951974

"Above all, they were not in a hurry. They made fewer speeches, and lived more meditatively and more at leisure, with companionship rather than motion for their solace. They had far fewer facilities than we have for the frittering away of thought, time, and life."

—Sir Winston S. Churchill
*Marlborough*

# CONTENTS

# PATHS OF DESIRE

Snakey green slide

Dead VW bus

BACK FORTY

Wild Wisteria

New Lawn

Sitting Around Corner

Little White Bird

New Lawn

The Long & Winding Path

Where the skunks eat grubby dinners

RDEN

Hedge fund saplings

1. New Back Bed
2. Norway Disgrace
3. Wounded Oak
4. Dogwoods
5. Venetian Wellhead
6. Surviving Hemlock
7. Old Brick Path
8. Defaced Buddha

# PROLOGUE

## *My Kind of Garden*

*"We love the things we love for what they are."*
—Robert Frost
"Hyla Brook"

This is not the story of a garden in the country—sprawling over several acres, shaded by an abundance of trees, moistened with the cool night air evaporating off a riffling stream, its beds of roses, lilies, pinks and perennials, herbs and vegetables, contained and protected in room after room built of ancient, crumbling brick, unfolding in an architecture of blooming, buzzing bounty. (As I imagine my country garden might look, had I countryside in my command.) Nor is this the story of an urban garden, a penthouse terrace, say, featuring a demure pas de deux of columnar cedar framing the entrance, set against the twinkling lights of boxy skyscrapers. Herbs striking a modern pose, too, if you please, in their stainless steel planters by the kitchen door.

This is the story of a more typical sort of garden, the sort of garden being planted all over the country, conventional, mundane, even: squeezed, stuffed, parched, repeated everywhere and anywhere in countless variations, full of the hobbling steps we take—and the big mistakes we make—when learning to do something. Beautiful, to my eye. Beloved. And I dare say that most people, pottering around on their small plots, feel exactly the same way about this kind of garden. This is the story of gardens in the suburbs, and more accurately, one garden in the suburbs. Mine.

This is the story of a garden I have tended, and not tended, over the course of the last fifteen years. It is a garden that has been marked and shaped by my young married life, by my life as the mother of two boys, by my life as a woman at the end of her marriage, having lost the urge to plant and nurture, and by my life as a woman once again happy to be gardening vigorously, full of zest and hope for the future, and, more important, pleasure in the moment, pleasure in the imprinting of some tiny part of the universe.

The garden lies in a small Westchester village that borders the northern edge of the Bronx in New York City. I have written about this garden, now and again, over the years, but I never stopped to take the measure of its larger plan, or traced its growth in any coherent way, or acknowledged all that it has taught me. And I never thought about what it meant to have a garden in the suburbs, what the things were that we suburban gardeners contend with that our country cousins do not.

Many gardening books describe, often vividly, how to do things in a garden: what to plant, and when to plant, and where to plant, and how to water and prune and feed and put down the plants. These books are useful, of course. They are good for the early winter evenings when I draw up lists of things I intend to put in my garden (but probably never will), when I try to sketch out an idea for a new way to shape a bed (and there I am promiscuous, for I leap happily and easily from fantasies of hard-edged plantings within a strict geometry to beds of soft, undulating lines).

Sometimes gardening books are simply beautiful to look at. I turn to that kind especially often in the middle of winter, when, if I am lucky enough to catch a train home from work while there is still some light out, everything is in the rueful shades of a sparrow's grays and browns. Those are the days when the air is cuttingly damp outside and crackling dry inside, when the beds are mud and even the evergreens are barely making the effort to stay true to type. Those are the days when I am haunted by the stark sight of bare limbs that want pruning, but nothing can, or should, be done. I turn to gardening books to wrap myself in hopeful dreams of early springtime, with its poignant warm spells, all too short-lived, or when I crave visions of early summer, in its exuberance of color. There it all is, the future, how life will be next season, next time around, in the garden; a life bathed in glowing, glossy, five-color promise on the rich pages I hold in my lap.

But the story I want to tell is not really about how my suburban garden looks, though that matters, and it certainly isn't about how to design and tend a suburban plot; I claim no wide mastery in that department and can impart only the knowledge culled from my small adventure. I wish I could describe a garden filled with rare treasure hoarded over years of exploration; I wish I could point slyly to the stunning *Meconopsis betonicifolia* I coaxed through difficult seasons, or the *Rodgersia podophylla* I carried over from England. The fact is, even if I had such specimens, I would never remember their names, for I am as hopeless with the names of plants as with the names of people. This affliction has grown worse with the years, and sometimes even the name of a familiar shrub, one that I have seen as often as I have seen my own children, eludes me (as, at times, do the names of my children). Rather, I'm mostly intrigued with the tale of how the garden feels, or said another way, how the garden makes me, and those who visit, feel.

Much of how a garden feels has to do with all the things that happen in the course of gardening, things that have little to do with plants or beddings. The arguments, the surprises, the mistakes, the delights, the laughs, the tears, the shortcuts, the long ways around—and the memories. Gardens are decidedly not just about the plants in them, or the way the plants are organized. And because the suburban garden begins as a blank slate, the effort of creation is more apparent than in those beds long ago carved out of a rolling, generous, seductive— and instructive—countryside. The country garden will follow the contours of the land; it will wrap itself round trees, or bank itself along rills; it will have room to stretch out and to carry you the distance. The suburban garden begins with nothing. Its contours are shaped by people—not just the gardener, but those who wander through, just visiting or lending a hand. The suburban garden is all about ushering nature back into the very plot of land from which it has been recently banished, then controlling and ordering it, the better to appreciate it and live with it. The stories a suburban garden will tell you are about birds and skunks, driveways and neighbors, fountains and furniture, dreams disappointed, then resurrected. And at its best, the suburban garden will become a place for enchantment, casting its gentle spell on all who pass through.

The experience of *being* in the garden is what preoccupies me, for I think that in and around and underneath all the decisions we make about shaping and planting, the most important part of what a garden does lies in the mysterious, subtle, nearly ineffable but heartfelt ways it stirs you to the depths of your soul. That is the magic of gardening. It is only when you are open-hearted in the garden that it can begin to show you what you need to do to take care of it. And what it can do for you. The trick, of course, is how to make that connection. Somehow, somewhere along the years, I did, with my unassuming suburban garden.

# ONE

# THE WALL FALLS DOWN

*"Absence my presence is, strangeness my grace."*
—Fulke Greville, Lord Brooke
"When all this All doth pass
from age to age"

I woke unusually early one morning, and, after a while of squirming deeper under the blankets, realized there would be no returning to my dreams. A violent storm had passed through the night; perhaps the commotion had stirred me from sleep. I rose from my bed and went down to the kitchen in my nightgown to make a cup of coffee. As it began to brew, I leaned on the counter, looking idly out the window at the back of the garden. For most of fifteen years, the first thing in the garden I saw every morning was a long, narrow bed fifteen feet from my kitchen door. That morning, as it had for all those years, my gaze came to rest on what I called the Back Bed. (I have a proclivity for naming things, and when I have to defend the habit, I refer the eye-rollers to Gertrude Jekyll, who, in her books, pointed out the convenience of such a practice and blithely christened every corner of her world.) The Back Bed was crammed with colorful annuals and soft perennials and fragrant herbs and flowering shrubs, full of the sweet things I had profusely, if indiscriminately, nurtured since I had moved into the house. It gave me great pleasure, every morning, to see how my plants had come through the night; to find the tender, spongy crowns of the sedum and the new shoots of bamboo cutting up from the rich, damp soil; to watch the glimmer of raindrops caught in the foxgloves; to see the clear, early light filter through the bloodred teardrops of the *Dicentra spectabilis;* to follow the rampage of the starry clematis as it strangled its way through its bedfellows; to trace the contagious flush across the tousled heads of the hydrangea. Less pleasing, but just as compelling, was my daily inspection of the ravages of the slugs chewing through the large, veiny leaves of the fragrant hosta (and why were none of these slugs attracted to the little saucers of beer in which they were meant to drown?); or my daily swipes at the frothy white sacs of scum spun by the spittlebugs along the thick stalks of rosemary. The Back Bed had a small, cozy, crazy-quilt charm, of the sort a child's drawing of a flower garden might suggest. In my first years as a gardener, I gave my heart to it all, so carelessly.

It was looking as if we would have a perfect summer day. An unusual and punishing heat wave had finally broken. Yet things seemed peculiar outdoors, that morning. Thinking I was definitely up too early, and my head was clouded, I poured a cup of coffee and stepped out the back door. My foot sank into two inches of mud. I picked up the hem of my long white nightgown. Well, I thought vaguely, looking around, the rain must have washed out a great deal of earth from somewhere. The pot of ponytail grass sitting on a low wall in front of me, with a wild blue morning glory entwined in its long, trailing mane, looked as filthy and ragged and matted as drowned Ophelia. The Back Bed was strangely askew; everything in it seemed to be slanting in an unusual manner, as if bowed down. The plants must be weighted with water, I reasoned; it must have been quite a storm. I took a step toward the bed, intending to give some of the branches a shake. The mud sucked the slipper right off my foot, but I took a few more sinking steps anyway, distracted enough not to notice the ooze between my toes.

So deep was my denial of what had happened that it was not until I was holding in my hand the tender, thickly pearled branch of a rose of Sharon—they have such soft, pliant wood—that I realized that the shrub was inclining toward me, bearing across its back the enormous weight of a long concrete retaining wall that had collapsed during the night.

As I stood, dumbfounded, in front of my poor rose of Sharon, the wall gave off a terrible cracking noise, followed by a deep groan, and then it heaved itself the rest of the way onto the Back Bed, crushing everything under it. My coffee cup slipped from my hand and shattered against a stone ledge. A wave of muddy water from the uphill neighbor's yard, which stood six feet higher than mine (hence the retaining wall), came tumbling off the concrete edge, and pooled around my feet.

All was quiet.

I stood still, shocked, unable to take in the devastation.

Fifteen years of tenderly, lovingly, making my bed, gone. Just like that.

How could a wall that had been standing nearly a hundred years simply fall over one night, without a warning? But it had. Was it a sign? An ill omen? What could it mean? A length of fifty feet of concrete, ten inches thick and standing five feet high, weighing tons, had split open at the base and toppled forward, smashing every shrub, every flower, every piece of statuary (and I confess there was a bit too much of that).

It was beyond repair. I was looking at a large catastrophe, exactly the sort of overwhelming mess that I am nearly incapable of handling. Raindrops glistened all around me, dripping slowly and gracefully off the tips of outstretched branches, their sparkling, casual beauty indifferent to the disaster I was facing. I stood alone, disheveled, my nightgown slipping off my shoulder, barefoot in the cool mud, nudging the shards of my coffee cup, a slipper embalmed at the kitchen door, and I began to laugh, hysterically.

That is how the story of this suburban garden begins. With the collapse of a wall. A retaining wall, naturally. What other sort of wall could collapse with such consequence?

The Back Bed had been a shambolic affair, but I was fond of it because it was the first bed I planted when I moved from Texas to New York with my husband and two-year-old son. The bed had been an attempt, a small one, to put my mark on a suburban garden that was nearly a hundred years old.

Something about that garden—and it was because of the garden that I had fallen in love with the house, though it, too, had a warm, simple beauty—implored me to come to its rescue. My first impression of the house was that it had been lost in an eccentric forest. The front yard, not even a quarter acre in size, was filled with gangly, gnarled, and twisting sassafras trees, dozens of them, a fast-growing, awkward tree that has no branching to speak of until the top of the trunk, several stories up. The dark, deeply grooved bark of the long, bare trunks is the main appeal of these trees. (The minty scent of the late-autumn leaves rotting on the ground is another.) Squatting at the feet of the trees were mounds of azaleas, some of them six or seven feet tall. I had always thought azaleas needed sun; these were basking in the dense shade. Thick ropes of English ivy snaked up the sides of the trees and hung in curtains from the branches. Swaths of the front walk, of a soft, crumbling old brick, had been swallowed by carpets of weedy grass and Virginia creeper. The front yard— flanked as it was by neighboring houses with carefully tended lawns, their politely discreet balls of shrubbery standing sentry by their front doors—was beguiling. There was no other front yard like it in town, as the realtor pointed out with disdain when we first saw the house. She helpfully suggested a chain saw.

Apart from the unusual front yard, which I was soon calling the Old Garden, as it had clearly been planted when the house was built nearly a hundred years earlier, the property featured a typical suburban side yard, not too interesting, with tall, straggly hemlocks arranged in a clumpy line, looking bedraggled; they had, years earlier, artfully blocked the house next door from view. There was the standard backyard, with its green lawn, an arrangement of shrubbery in danger of being strangled by bittersweet vines, and several trees—a few aging beauties among them. A crumbling black asphalt driveway, splotched and patched, bordered the other side of the house; it had a slight pitch to it, as my house was about five feet higher than the road that ran in front of it—just as the houses behind were a great deal higher than my own. The neighborhood straddled the side of a slope. The whole effect was enchanting. After months of searching, we had finally found our new home. And I had come into possession of my first garden. I took up its care with great seriousness.

My plot of land occupies less than half an acre overall, and that is being generous with the measurements. The kind of suburb in which I live does not feature big yards. To get that, you have to move deeper into the countryside, and once you are working four or five acres of land, you are no longer truly in the suburbs, or at least, not the old-fashioned kind. You may be in the new burbs, driving a car to get a bottle of milk. You don't recognize your neighbors, your children are not safe riding their bicycles in the narrow, winding streets, and there are no sidewalks on which to push a stroller. You probably live in northern Connecticut. Or Idaho.

The suburbs, as I see it, are places from which we have short commutes, by train or by car, to the work that enables us to afford living in them. We live there because we want to live in houses, as opposed to city apartments; because the public schools are still viable choices for our children; because our children can play in the yard, and have swing sets and soccer fields and nice, clean skateboard ramps, however oxymoronic that might be (moronic, my younger son would say; he is a passionate skateboarder who wishes we lived in an office park surrounded by fields of concrete). We spend years with the same friends; we get to work quickly and easily, even if traffic snarls along the main arteries, but when we leave the office we succumb to a delicious feeling of escape. Usually we live in the suburbs because we were once suburban children. And because we can create our own gardens to tend.

It is imperative that your city-dwelling friends look down their noses at your suburbanite ways and middle-class, escapist values. Gardens, indeed. Though I commute to an office in midtown Manhattan every day, urbanites always ask me, with smug concern, whether I ever "get into the city," so that we might manage a dinner together. Suburbanites think, with their own smug superiority, that city folks have lost touch with the good life, and are selfishly sacrificing their children's need to swing on swing sets for their own need to wear black all the time. Soon enough, though, you make your peace with your choice of where to live, and stop worrying about any of this.

In most suburbs, people don't particularly care who you are, in terms of what you do. Allegiances are formed around altogether different occupations, such as raising the children, or raising money, or building libraries and art centers. Friendships are sparked by shared interests that lie in realms far from workday lives. How many friends have I made, since living in the suburbs, simply because our children were in the same class, or on the hockey team together? (I suppose a similar thing happens in the city to people who walk dogs in the park at the same time every day.) People in real suburbs live close by one another and share property lines and grocery lines, fight over boundaries, compete for seats on governing boards, pass each other amicably (or not) on the sidewalk, and toot a horn in greeting in the streets. At the train station, I recognize people with whom I have shared a ride into the city over the years and nod hello, whether or not we have ever been introduced. Standing on the platform, waiting, I have watched people age, or grow ill, or swell with pregnancy; I have recognized the children of commuters in the curve of a smile or the stoop of a shoulder, watched them joining a mother or father on the train to go to their own first jobs, carrying on after the parent retires his or her place on the train. And every spring I have watched people proudly carry from their gardens to their offices large bunches of lilacs, or daffodils, or branches of forsythia lovingly bundled in soggy newspaper and foil and held tight with string to keep in the moisture, as we suburban children were taught to do by our mothers.

As a person who loved living in New York City, where I had gone after graduating from college, it was a struggle to accustom myself to a house in the suburbs. That struggle was immensely relieved by my garden, for that was a place in which I felt I could connect to the pleasure of a suburban life. The day we moved into our new house, the neighbors from across the street greeted us with a freshly baked apple pie. This was my first taste of suburban boosterism; I accepted it cheerfully. Little did I suspect that there was a darker side—but that came later. Within days of unpacking our boxes, I went to work in the Old Garden in front of the house. I was determined to release it from the vines that were threatening to choke off life, and restore it to a thriving maturity. The previous owners, and there had been only two in nearly a hundred years, had had strong ideas about gardens, as I could tell by what they had left behind. Even though things were overrun when I moved in, the basic contours of the garden all around the house were fairly transparent, bold and demanding. I yielded immediately to the allure, and the demands, of the Old Garden, and threw myself into the work with great devotion.

At first, I added very little that was new to the grounds. I figured I didn't have the expertise to know what to do. I had some vague sense that an understanding of how a garden should look lies more in a feeling of recognition than an abrupt imposition of a fantasy onto the land. In other words, as my garden grew on me, I could take my time growing into my garden.

This process is often referred to, in a by now rather wearisome manner, as consulting the genius of a place. Perhaps Alexander Pope's dictum is still worthwhile, conceptually, but it seems more appropriate to the large country garden, for which it was intended, where genius would be grand, as genius ought to be, and roam freely, playing a sort of hide-and-seek with the gardener. Locating the genius—to say nothing of arranging the consultation—requires hours, if not days and years, of the peace and quiet necessary to such a contemplative pursuit. But suburban gardeners labor with more than the song of birds in their ears—planes buzz overhead, the trains rattle through town, traffic whizzes nearby, fire trucks wail, tires screech and horns blow, the impassioned voices of children come through the shrubbery, laughing, shrieking, fighting, and crying.

My garden may have needed a genius to define it, but, for better and for worse, it was going to have to settle for me. Every suburban garden requires, from time to time, the creative, willful imposition of its owner. Carved as it is out of some old, wealthy, landed family's sprawling estate (because the wealth has trickled away and they are cash poor, land rich), or parceled out of a farmstead (because the profit from selling vegetables and eggs is long gone), the suburban garden begins with genius having been wiped out. The suburban garden starts its life as a construction site. There is simply not enough room to maneuver on the plot of land to build the house without destroying the surroundings. Rubble, rabble, dirt, and dust are all the beleaguered genius has left behind. But the new house, stark, fresh, proud, and probably (these days) too big, is standing. Only then is it time to think about the garden. Or, as they say, the landscaping.

Most suburban gardens begin life with so-called foundation plantings. These are the little petticoats of plants, the bloomers of shrubbery, that we wedge in around the foundation of the house, as if we were embarrassed by the honest, forthright materials used to shore up our dreams. Foundation plantings, which include such things as banks of clipped yew, or ranks of azalea, or ruffles of hosta all in a line (though evergreens are preferable), or boxwood (if you are fortunate), form a ring of greenery that is meant, eventually, to cover low rims of brick, concrete, or stone (if you are fortunate in your foundations, as well). The house is meant to look like a big, beneficent hen, roosting on her nest of shrubbery.

Long before planting out the foundation, though, the developer will have buried the boulders and rubble and debris that are part and parcel of any construction site, with its excavations of basements or swimming pools, and carted in loads of dirt, dumped it over the whole mess, and then, as if icing a cake, spread a fine layer of topsoil whose rich, dark color looks like dirt ought to look. Surface beauty. Upon presentation to the marketplace this concoction will, of course, be entirely seeded with grass.

The developer is not thinking about landscaping, exactly, much less gardening. Nor should he be. He is thinking about curb appeal and resale value. He will have carved out a path to the front door, usually tracing a straight line up to the house from the sidewalk, and another path from the kitchen door to the driveway. The driveway will probably be poured—a thick, black, bubbling, pungent asphalt—over the same path the bulldozers have tamped down during construction, which is to say the shortest distance from the street

to the work area, which is invariably next to the garage.
Having demarcated entrances and exits, he will plop a tree
or two on either side of the front lawn; trees, in small doses,
and not perilously close to the house, are still considered a
worthwhile investment, enhancing the value of the property.
These garden things are all part of the basic package; they
come with the house, so to speak. This has been the case
since suburban neighborhoods were first developed in this
country; look at the pictures of the proud new houses featured in magazines like *House & Garden* for a nascent middle-
class eighty years ago—even by 1940, only 15 percent of the
American population lived in suburbs—and you see the
same sort of landscaping.

The new owner, just moving in, might decide to lay down
a patio, or build a deck over a sloping yard, or put up a fence
or a stone wall, or terrace a hillside. This activity is closely followed by the planting of some gaily colored flowers, and a few
more trees, one perhaps in commemoration of ownership, so
that far into the future, when the tree towers over the house,
the original owners will drive by their old home (for no
human stays planted very long) and say fondly, wistfully,
"We put that tree in the ground the day we moved into the
place." Even better is to be able to add: ". . . and the seedling
came in the mail, that's how small it was."

Thus begins the life of a suburban garden. Mine, laid out
around 1910, took shape as a variation on the form, due to
the idiosyncrasies of its first owners. In some ways, it does
not depart from the norm, of decades ago or yesterday. The
rubble is buried beneath the soil, as I have learned every
time I have tried to dig a sizable hole. The drive comes
straight up from the street, though the garage is a building
separate from the house; at the beginning of the twentieth

century no one dreamed of sharing his house with a car, as there were five automobiles in America in 1895. In fact, my garage, like most of the old ones in this town, was originally a stable; men took their horse and buggy to the train station. The foundation of the house was rimmed with azaleas. But somehow, when it came to the front yard, the first owner of the house got sidetracked.

I learned something of the history of my garden from a chance encounter. I was in the front, one day, sawing away on a large dead limb of an azalea, covered head to toe in dirt and bark dust, my hair thick with twigs, sweating profusely and happily. I was jolted out of my rapture by the sound of a woman's voice, calling out, "Excuse me, *excusez-moi,* please, *pardonnez-moi,* hello?" I peered out from under the canopy of the azalea to see, standing on the sidewalk below me, an attractive, middle-aged woman, with a decidedly bohemian flare, her hair piled up and pinned on top of her head, puffing a cigarette; trailing and bobbing behind her, as if tethered, was a much younger, and much distracted, dark-eyed man. The whole picture was too chic.

I wiped off my face, straightened my shirt, brushed off my arms, and pulled off my rubber gloves. (Yes, I wear gloves; I don't go in for the current machisma of bare-handed grappling with nature. The previous fall, I had wantonly pulled up and used a tough vine to bundle the weeds and branches I had pruned—how convenient, I remember thinking, this vine is in endless supply; no need to go to the house for the twine. I did not recognize the toxic cordage I held in my bare hands, and the bout of poison ivy that followed, with me tearing the skin from my arms, ended my romance with digging my fingers into the earth. The earth always ends up in the gloves anyway.

Those of us too stupid to recognize trouble before we get into it have to protect ourselves.)

The woman on the sidewalk introduced herself as the granddaughter of the original owner of the house. She explained that she was visiting from her home in Paris, and had come to see the old place out of nostalgia for her childhood. My visitor stubbed out her cigarette on the sidewalk and threw a shawl dramatically over her shoulder. I invited her to join me in the woods, and she and the lover (as I imagined him) clambered up the few feet of the rocky ledge that kept my front yard from collapsing into the street. The pair settled themselves on a big boulder, after I brushed it clean for them.

"My grandparents were wealthy," Mademoiselle said, putting her handbag down in the ivy, crossing her legs, lighting another cigarette. "They built this house for themselves, the whole thing for just the two of them." She gave her lover a sideways glance; this story seemed as much for his appreciation as mine. He stood and began to pace through the pachysandra. Back and forth, back and forth. What a restless soul.

Her grandfather had made his fortune in cotton, she said, and was living on the Upper East Side of New York City when the sprawling Pell estate ten miles away, bought from the Siwanoy Indians in 1654, began to be subdivided. Eventually, her grandfather's fortunes rising, he decided to look for a summer house (which in those days meant a house close enough to the city so that the entire household could move there from May through October, while the breadwinner commuted to earn a living). Her grandfather had ridden the train up through Westchester along the shore of Long Island Sound, my visitor explained—tugging on her lover's leash a bit, to my relief, as he had begun to stray farther through the trees. Grandfather had boarded the train at Grand Central

Station, his newspaper tucked under his arm, and settling in, unfolded the paper and began to read. (In those days reading *The New York Times* was a much more straightforward affair; it wasn't bloated with so many sections.) He arrived at the end of the *Times* just as the train was pulling into a pretty little station surrounded by saplings, and, judging that to be an adequate commute, he had gotten off at what was a fairly new development, strolled down the street a couple of blocks, and purchased this plot and built his house. So went the family lore.

I nodded in appreciation, and remarked that I, too, had noticed the commute to be the perfect length for the paper; it had never occurred to me that I would have paced myself through the paper at whatever length of commute I had been allocated.

The visitor continued. What my husband and I considered to be a five- or six-bedroom house had been designed to accommodate Grandpapa and his wife—and their staff, four in-help, my visitor said, pointedly using this term of art. When we had moved in I had found the original blueprints for the house rolled up in an enormous closet upstairs, and remarked on two master bedrooms on the second floor, adjoined by a morning room, to which, as the granddaughter told me, every morning breakfast was hoisted via dumb-waiter by a servant in the kitchen. (What an appealing idea. But my life was turning out a bit differently. I could not maintain his-and-her bedrooms. By then I had two sons. And their baby-sitter. And the husband's research assistant. And two offices in the house. As for the dumbwaiter, I had had it sealed off when a toddler had somehow unlatched the door and hidden himself in the cage—thank goodness he had not crawled into an empty shaft.) The third-floor plan identified a trunk room—there was no attic (all the same I had never heard of a trunk room, and loved the romance it evoked, of packing for a monthlong sea voyage aboard an ocean liner); a large butler's room—"Yes, yes, the butler was married to the cook," said the granddaughter; a small chauffeur's room, and an even smaller maid's room. Indeed, the floors in the rooms upstairs were an unremarkable, yellowing pine, an abrupt change from the rich, gorgeous, amber tones of the fruitwood flooring that had been lavished on the rest of the house.

Her grandparents had been avid collectors of fine French furniture, my visitor said, stretching her neck (and eyeing her lover) with some vanity, and a little gilt bench that had been perched under the arched window of the library was so valuable that it was now residing in the Metropolitan Museum of Art. Had I ever seen it there? (I was not quite sure.) Did I have a library? (I had a lot of books; did that qualify?) Did I have a proper bench in the arched room? (Proper?)

I was delighted to hear a little bit about the house, though feeling slightly grumpy at how the class structure had shifted, and not in my favor; the history gave my home a new dimension. Any house ought to be well considered in daydreams of new gardens; it has much more of a bearing on the nature of a garden than we like to think. After all, the house will always be the largest thing in the suburban garden.

The granddaughter was pleased to see that the sassafras trees had not been cleared away; she remembered playing in those woods, and she was complimentary about the size and health of the azaleas. That touched my own vanity, as I had spent countless hours repairing the damage done by a careless, last-minute, house-on-the-market-too-long-no-offers pruning job, in which some of the plants had been sheared and bobbed to within an inch of their lives, in the (sadly) typical suburban manner of those parts. Probably the realtor had advised the owners to let in more light.

Her grandmother had been the gardener, my visitor said, and decided to leave the stand of sassafras intact. The entire neighborhood had once been wooded, as the land had never been farmed and was renowned for its excellent quail hunting. The grandmother had planted many things under the trees, starting with the azaleas, masses of them. (Our biggest surprise during our first spring in the house were the drifts of white blossoms under the trees; they looked like banks of snow, and people drove up and parked and asked to have their picture taken among the azaleas. Over the years I identified Delaware Valley whites, Palestrinia, with its faint green-stained throat, the dwarf Ptarmigan.) The grandmother had added larger types of rhododendron, and some *Pieris japonica*—"White Cascade"— and under all the shrubs she had laid a carpet of ivy and pachysandra, streaked here and there with trout lily and jack-in-the-pulpit and bunches of delicately striped painted ferns. As her grandparents were called the Whites, my visitor said, everything they planted had to bear white flowers, even the trees. Only white was allowed. And they named the place Whitewood.

I began to wonder when the naming of houses and gardens had come to sound so pretentious. The granddaughter and her lover got into a heated tête-à-tête. Whitewood. What would have happened had their names been Black? Would my own garden be wilting and browning?

My thoughts drifted to other house names. I pondered the mystery of why so many wealthy men called their new houses Toad Hall; hadn't they read the book? Didn't they see the joke they were making of themselves? Or had their mothers read *The Wind in the Willows* to them when they were children, so that somehow Toad came off as a more adorable and inspiring creature than he really was? Or perhaps the wealthy men simply wanted to crawl back into their mamas' laps?—My visitor interrupted my train of thought with a question about the train schedule; she refused offers of refreshment, and seemed to have retreated from further curiosity about the state of the house and my possessions. Or perhaps she had been drawn into the vacant, agitated air of her lover. The stroll down memory lane was called to an abrupt halt, and the pair headed for the station. I went back to my work in the azaleas, thrilled, a little haunted, and certainly vexed by the sudden apparition of the Original Gardener, Mrs. White, with her exacting standards and high expectations and gilt benches and many servants.

My job of restoring the Old Garden was to consume many years—it will never end. Many a time I have thought about Mrs. White, wondering if she had started the colony of Solomon's seal that rose up one year, if she had ever imagined the azalea would be large enough to tent her cozily within. Wondering, too, if she had longed to toil in the dirt, but was inhibited by the proprieties of her time and class. She had undoubtedly had gardeners of her own—and there have been plenty of days when I envied her that help.

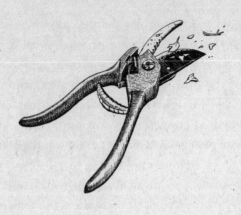

# GROUNDS FOR RENOVATION

*"The great way is very level;*
*But people delight in torturous paths."*
—Lao-tzu
*Te Tao Ching*

O
ne day, soon after we had moved into the house, I walked out the back door from the kitchen and saw a couple of mysterious plants poking, with great determination, their way out from the edge of the driveway. Fugitives from a buried bed. I had never seen such plants in my life. Two strong stalks of dusty green with thick leaves ranked up the sides, they grew taller and taller—I felt like Jack watching his beans rise—until they reached a height of five feet. The stalks were noble and erect, as if they were flagpoles from which

would unfurl heraldic banners. Then the stalks began to bloom, a profusion of blossoms up and down their length of a mottled, breathtaking, unnameable blue. A Botticelli blue. A blue close to the clearest depths of southern seas, or the celestial orbs frescoed on the ceilings of old churches. And then again, a blue that lay closer to the inky mauve of a slow dusk. The color was shifting, changeable. This was my introduction to the aristocratic delphinium. For years afterward, I searched the garden catalogs to find a flower that resembled the ones that seemed to have come down to my backyard from the heavens; I figured out that they were a hybrid of the *elatum* group, but I have faltered in finding the color, which hovers elusively, winking at me, somewhere between the "Blue Nile" and "Bruce." It is like that blue spot in the middle of the darkness behind your eyeballs, the so-called Blue Pearl at the heart of meditation, that the seeker finds only upon transcending time and place and the need to scratch an itch. I have read about it, but will never find it. I had seen the mythic delphinium; I was soon to lose it forever. Those flowers that appeared at the back of the driveway came bearing a message, I was sure. It was time to start a new bed in the back. That was how we came to rip out the parking lot.

Parking lot? you say. It was an unusual landscaping feature, to say the least, for a suburban backyard—at least in those days. It was an extension of the driveway, tucked around behind the kitchen at the back of the house, paved and fenced off from the rest of the yard. A beautiful old pink rose, with trunks as thick as my wrists, spilled over the fence rails. The previous owner, who had had a sister and several grown children living with her, had needed to accommodate many cars. We owned but one car, so we pried up the asphalt and replaced it with flagstone, and, shoving some dirt up against the ungainly concrete

wall that seemed to be the only thing keeping the uphill neighbor's garage from sliding into our yard, we created a slightly
raised bed, held in place with a low stone wall. The neighbor's
garage—which was actually a beautiful old wreck of a stone
carriage house—loomed above my new garden area, the Back
Bed, and its granite walls trapped the heat of the winter sun
and kept the climate behind the house mild.

The Back Bed was about four feet deep and twenty-seven
feet long. As it was in the sunniest part of the yard, it readily
took on whatever perennials I could squeeze into it; they
thrived. The patio off the kitchen instantly became the summer dining room, where I could gaze happily at the new
flowers. What's more, the Back Bed had the advantage of
partly shrouding more than half of the band of concrete retaining wall that ran partway across the back of the property—and
what a nasty wall it was. It had nothing to recommend it save
for its Atlas-like devotion to holding up the neighbors' world.
It did not even seem to weather properly, but stayed the same
mealy and uninteresting color through every season.

(Over the following years I would try to further mask the
wall with various covers and creepers, the unfortunate
*Euonymus fortunei,* or wintercreeper, and English ivy,
*Hedera helix,* but though all these plants were considered
invasive, they seemed to bake right off in the hot sun, as if
my wall were repellent even to a pest. Finally, years after the
creation of the Back Bed, I would plant a clematis, *montana,*
at one end of the wall, simply because I had ordered too
much of it for a different spot. I had no hope for its survival,
as I had always thought that clematis was a fragile, fussy
thing. But it was so wildly contented with its spot at the end
of the wall that within a year I was able to train it down the
length of concrete; it cascaded off the top. It bloomed pro-

fusely every spring, its small white flowers glowing into the night, and I thought I had triumphed over the wall, until one year, after a severe—and accidental—pruning, the clematis became demented, and began to twine its way into everything else in the bed, haywire, strangling whatever it could. I had never seen such a coy, robust invader. The wall, clearly, was cursed. I decided to ignore it. Little did I know of the perils of ignoring trouble.)

With guidance from a Design Expert at a nearby nursery, I planted a row of shrubs in the Back Bed, to pick up the line of some shrubs that were already in place along the back of the yard—three hydrangea, because of the two old hydrangea at the back of the house, which bloomed a hard, almost green white late in the summer, then tarnished, fading into a beautiful rosy blush of powdery old age. In the new bed I planted a standardized form; I felt that would look more delicate, balletic, sending its sprays of flowers twirling from a central trunk. Because there were already some in the yard, I alternated the hydrangea with two althea, or rose of Sharon, shrubs that would grow in a vase shape that I admired. Their flowers also came late in the season; they were white with a crimson center, and there seemed an endless supply of them. The shrubs looked so small and forlorn, once they were in, that I decided to fill the spaces between them with perennials. And so I squeezed into the Back Bed anything and everything I liked from the catalogs, augmented by supplies from the local nursery. Lavender, rosemary, phlox, hollyhock, foxglove, mint—oh, the mistakes I made—sedum, daisies. I spent lavishly, extravagantly; I gardened licentiously.

I had been intimidated by flowers, at first, but then was seduced by the catalogs. I loved reading the names of things, the way it felt to say them, mouthing my way into the private language of the gardener. *Monarda,* with its swelling, soothing, matronly vowels—bee balm. *Echinacea,* sounding like the very sneeze the coneflower was meant to ward off. The silvery *artemisia,* surely a fairy's flower. *Campanula,* ringing in morning devotions. Over the next few years, I ordered and crammed and moved and tended and lost and yanked and killed. You can never know what will work in your garden until you try it. And discipline of design is harder won, and all the more satisfying, when it has conquered the instinct for profligacy. My hand would eventually grow firmer, my eye more sophisticated. But neither was of interest to me in the early days of gardening.

In my first years with the Back Bed, I was a blissfully ignorant gardener, and, although it was masked by the extravagant planting, I was also quite insecure. I put in the shrubs to give "structure," as I had an idea that shrubs made bones, and bones were virtuous. I copied what was already in the yard so that I could feel safe about my choices. And at the same time I was riotously haphazard; sloppy, really, troweling in anything that caught my eye, or ear, with no regard to color, size, habit, or overall effect.

I sometimes wished I could have been like those professional landscape designers who go to a paint store, mix chips of color together until they find a pleasing combination, and then plant accordingly, sticking to the plan no matter what the temptations of the nursery. The best that could be said of my efforts was that I had tender feelings about whatever went into the Back Bed. Eventually I grew to appreciate that a solicitous touch was at least as important as a ruthless eye.

One day in early spring, a few months before the collapse of the retaining wall, workmen began to mill around the stone carriage house. The house had been neglected for years, which gave it charm, I thought, but also made it an appealing home for skunks and rats. Not so charming. I watched from my kitchen window over the next few months as the men rebuilt the crumbling chimney, shored up the foundations, trimmed the roof in gleaming copper gutters. They replaced rotting window sashes, then replaced the old glass (one of the panes shattered by a son's errant—so I was told—baseball). I could peer into the bottom floor and see a furnace being dismantled and a new one being assembled. Electricians arrived, and stringy tangles of charred wire were removed and neat coils of shiny wire brought in.

I had new neighbors.

One morning, I woke to the grinding, scraping noise of bulldozers, and the sound of dynamite blasting rock out of the ground.

The new neighbors had ambitions.

The carriage house was the least of it. The main structure was an elaborate, four-story, stone-and-stucco Victorian layer cake of a house, one of the oldest in town, dating from the 1890s, swagged with rotting porches, boasting a gorgeous old slate roof of a soft, tarnished silver color, the loss of whose shingles was highly entertaining, if you were lucky enough to catch a showing. The slates would dislodge themselves, slide slowly down the slope of the roof, gather speed, and careen madly off the edge to the driveway far below, shattering deliciously. The house had been standing empty for a long time, caught in a muddle of estates and lawyers and distant relatives; its previous owner, a reclusive, eccentric, wealthy old woman who, it was said, kept all her money in brown paper bags in the closets, had died, alone in the house, years earlier. The house was now coming back to life, teeming with carpenters, masons, electricians, plumbers, and every other manner of helpful man.

And then began the assault on the grounds.

An old Victorian fountain, three-tiered, with dolphins and maidens holding pan upon pan over their heads, was removed. Oh, no! The paths to the carriage house were rerouted, graveled, and edged in Belgian block (that ubiquitous, stony status symbol). Trees were taken down, making room for the swing set (how many swing sets did one street need?), and shrubs removed—but the new owners had not even moved into the house yet—how could they know what they were taking out? Why hadn't they asked me? I had been watching that garden grow for over a decade! I understood it.

For weeks I heard blasting and drilling and groaning and grinding and buzzing. I reflected, wistfully, that for the last five years, I had been doodling plans for the renovation of my own property—enhancing the Old Garden, reorganizing the Back Bed, drawing pictures of new beds that would grace the other parts of the yard, especially the side yard, dawdling about fixing the driveway. Daydreaming, and doing nothing at all. Uphill, the neighbors hadn't even moved in, and the garden had been wrenched, with great decisiveness—at great expense—into an elaborate renovation.

My husband and I had divorced six years earlier and I had decided to stay in the house. Just before my husband left, I had shoehorned a last perennial into the Back Bed, half-heartedly pruned some azaleas in the Old Garden, and then simply given up the effort. For the next few years, I spent not another penny on the garden; I worked not another hour. I took some comfort in watching the garden take care of itself, for a season or two, in the sad days that followed the breakup of our family home—the shrubs smothering the threatening weeds with luxuriant new growth, the perennials letting loose a dazzling display of flowers, the sedum presenting as rich and burnished a bouquet as it ever had. Then the ivy began to creep up into the sassafras again, bittersweet twined into the hydrangea, the camellia took on a woebegone air, and I let it all go. Still, I felt fiercely protective of the garden, and could not imagine leaving it to the mercy of the next buyer, who might want what the realtor had called "curb appeal" and move in with that chain saw. I would never have been able to live in the same town as that garden and not watch over it. I intended to stay.

But I put off further alterations, though they were certainly needed. The Back Bed grew shabby. The Old Garden was clotted. In the side of the yard, the fifty-year-old hemlocks had been growing scraggly and dying. It was a dismal sight. The garden was now mine only in the sense that I owned it. I watched as it went into a gentle decline. I went with it.

In the next few years my confidence in my ability to ever manage the place again was steadily eroding, and I had begun to entertain thoughts of downsizing. The Boys and I would take evening walks past the local realtor's storefront office, and we would browse through the listings pictured in the windows. After reading all the notices carefully, the Boys would turn to me with sad faces. "Please, Mom, please don't downsize." They were rather poignant. "You are in the original house. You will never find anything like the original garden. You love your garden. We love the original house. We don't want to move."

So of course we did not move. But the fantasy that I might, someday, find a new garden to tend gave me an excuse, as if heartbreak were not reason enough, not to spend another penny on the grounds. Every once in a while, in a rush of affectionate memory for my old feeling about gardening, I doodled thoughts of what I would do on the property, if I were to allow myself to feel joy in it again. But I also kept a running tabulation, in my daydreams, of the cost, both financial and emotional, of adding more, cleaning it up, refreshing it—and deliberately making its gardens mine.

The elements in my calculations changed, over the years. I wouldn't spend the money because I was changing jobs; because no one else cared; because I was single; because the Boys were only there half of every week, so they wouldn't enjoy it enough (as if they had ever noticed it all); because I had to support myself; because I was too tired and too sad; because I was too busy; because I might move. Really, though, I had become afraid to deepen my roots. I had become afraid to care too much about my garden, or my house. What good did it do, to care? I was afraid to commit. I was locked in an ambivalent embrace—the worst kind.

By the time my new neighbors started their garden alterations, the calculus of noncommittal was quite refined. The Boys were growing up so fast. The oldest was about to leave home for college—for a while, "about to leave" meant in several years, then it was in a couple of years, and then, overnight, it was next year. He would be abandoning the garden—why bother to change anything? His brother trailed four years behind, so it was true that he would be around to enjoy the garden a bit longer. It is lovely to read stories about children who appreciate gardens, who gather up flowers in their little arms, bury their little noses in the fragrant blossoms, and trip and skip into the house to present their blowsy bouquets to their mothers. Those children like to weed; they are the children in books. When did a skateboarder ever care about flowers? My younger son wanted ramps, not beds.

My daydreams cost me nothing—a little agitation, perhaps, but no more. While the neighbors blasted and buzzed, I went on doodling. A new bed here, some new trees there, how about a fountain?—I had always wanted a fountain. Then I put my dreams aside.

One day the buzzing and blasting stopped, and the new neighbors moved in. All was quiet for a few weeks, until the stormy night when the wall fell down.

# THREE

# HELPFUL MEN

*"The secret of life is to have a task, something you devote your entire life to. . . . And the most important thing is—it must be something you cannot possibly do!"*
—Henry Moore

When the retaining wall toppled, I was so upset I could not do a thing about it for weeks. All I did was fret and worry. What did it mean that my retaining wall had toppled? I had been in that house for fifteen years without any such disaster. How bad an omen was this? What were the gods trying to tell me? Had I ignored warning signs? Was I ignoring other signs, about even bigger things? How on earth would I find someone to help me fix the mess?

Of course, the wall would have to be replaced, and of

course that was going to cost a fortune. Maybe I wouldn't replace the Back Bed. Maybe I would just continue to ignore the garden altogether. But I had once loved that Back Bed. I had always enjoyed looking at it, no matter what its desuetude. What should I do? On it went, the constant whine.

Luckily, it had been a mild spring, and I had had a couple of months to enjoy the terrace. I was conscious that I was finally bestirring myself, coming out of years of lassitude, beginning to live in the garden again.

That brings us to the matter of the True Love. And, though it gives me the dubious pleasure of bringing in a character who was on his way out—intent on leaving—I suppose this is as good a place as any to introduce one of the more influential, and troublesome, and lovable, fellows in the life of my garden. He had been in and out of my life in the most agreeable and disagreeable ways over the previous years. We had spent some happy moments in the garden, and he had done much to revive my enthusiasm for it with the delight he took in its charms. But the True Love was, sadly for me (and for him, too, if he would only realize it), in a phase of retreat by the time the wall collapsed, and it often crossed my mind, in the weeks that followed the calamity, that there must have been some connection between the havoc both forces, flooding rains and tears, were wreaking. Still, he had lifted the sodden edge of my torpor, roused me from dormancy, and helped me acknowledge and enjoy the blessings right before my eyes. A garden needs true love to get it going.

Just the day before the storm, I had had a lovely dinner with friends on the back terrace; we were cooking steaks when the first drops of rain fell. We moved the grill under the protection of a cheery red umbrella, and then we squeezed in under its shelter while a dazzling drizzle fell around us. A gentle beginning, indeed, for such a destructive storm. Little did I know it was to be my last dinner by the Back Bed.

It was well into the summer before I finally got around to calling stonemasons for bids on rebuilding the wall, perhaps even extending it farther along the back of the garden. When the first estimate came in, I nearly fainted. Eighty thousand dollars? Surely the mason had misunderstood. I did not want to build a new house. Just a wall.

"I know, lady," he said. "People used to build stone walls everywhere. Your town is full of them, stone walls all over the place. A dime a dozen. My grandfather, my father, they built many of them. Came over from the Old Country, from Italy, to build walls. Lots of people used to know how to build walls. But there aren't many of us left. We have to charge more. Who can pay is the rich people, the really rich people. Not the regular people. You should see the walls I'm building in Bedford, in Salem, in Chappaqua," he said, rattling off the names of Westchester's tonier preserves. "Miles of stone walls, I'm building. They love my walls, the rich people. I love those jobs."

I could tell I was going back to concrete, and wondered crankily how the wealthy White family, with its butler in the attic and its furniture at the Met, had ever gotten into concrete in the first place. Why couldn't they have put in a proper stone wall way back then? Then I began to think of the miles of walls at the True Love's country house, and envy crept down my spine. Gardeners are a jealous and covetous tribe. That the grass is greener on the other side is not metaphorical; it is reality. Nothing is ever good enough, and gardeners live in an eternal fantasy of a time when things were better, or will be better, in their own garden, and as for other people's gardens, well, if I broadcast money like fertilizer, I, too, could have all the many things I wanted. Which gets us to envy's alter ego: disdain. No one else's garden is really good enough, either.

In my typical sideways approach I decided, stonemasons being out of the question, to tackle the building of the wall by starting with the plans for a New Back Bed. I figured that vivid fantasies of floriferous bounty would get me through the building of the wall. Besides, I would always much rather discuss plants than bricks.

Enter Leonard, the first and most Helpful Man to come into this phase of my life. (And in my neck of the woods, I am sorry to observe, that's all there were in the service department—men. Plenty of them unhelpful, some helpless. The trick, by the way, to happy suburban life as a single woman— or a woman married to a hapless man—is to find the Helpful Men. Sometimes I have pangs of mortification at my dependence on them, but mostly I feel a defiant slavishness to their whims and fancies, especially when it comes to setting timetables and prices.) I came to rely on Leonard during what turned out to be, unexpectedly and delightfully, the year during which I was to make the entire garden mine.

First, though, the Helpful Man had to make it his. Leonard was the self-described owner and CEO of the local nursery, Lieb's Nursery and Garden Center. He came over and took a good look around.

"What a mess," he said helpfully. "Look at that damn thing. Concrete? Just broke off? Just like that? I don't know. That's strange. Must have been water. That doesn't just happen, just like that. And I can tell you've got a lot of plants under that slab. A lot of plants."

Of course he could tell. I had bought them from his nursery.

"You know, my grandfather probably put in most of the stuff in the front of the house," he said. This I had never heard, but it made sense; the Old Garden was full of mature shrubs. "He started the business. Family business. I'm the third generation. A lot of responsibility on my shoulders, with a family business. A lot of history. My brother is a landscape architect. But he isn't interested in the plants, in the soil. He is an academic. He takes *classes* in garden design. He makes *drawings*. Nice drawings. He reads *books* about gardening. He knows things. I keep telling him, when are you going to get a real job? Come help me out? *Work* in the garden. And he says, When would I have time to study, if I worked at the nursery? Well. That's my brother. I like doing gardens. I like digging and planting and feeding and pruning."

Of course I liked Leonard.

I had begun to observe that, among the people who loved gardens, there was something of a divide between those who appreciated and those who planted; those who hired and those who dug; those who studied and those who got dirty. I needed a garden lover of the hands-on variety.

"Don't worry," Leonard said. "Everything will be fine." (Little did I know, yet, that this was the mantra of the Helpful Man, to be repeated, with relentless conviction and a great deal of falsetto enthusiasm, around their high-strung, bill-paying female clients.) "We'll save what we can," he said. "I have a friend who can help you with the wall, by the way."

Leonard had grown up working at the nursery, and like many men who lived around my town during their child-hoods, he had never left, and had taken over the family trade. He had an elaborate network of Helpful Men, and he was not shy about calling on them to do some work. Suddenly all the people who had never bothered to return my calls began to show up at my door. I would come home at times to find them having little confabs on the driveway, their enormous trucks purring quietly, waiting. The plumber, the electrician, the builder: most of them had been friends in high school and, I noticed, most of them seemed barely out of school. I had entered the period in life in which one becomes dependent on the kind of people we call children. When, though, had I gotten that old?

Most of the time, I've begun to think, you just need someone else to give you a good push out of life's crises, to get you going again. It is confidence-inspiring to listen to other people talk about all the things they know how to do. Especially when they will do them for you.

I gave up on the stonemasons completely and hired Leonard's friend to rebuild the wall. We chose a concrete block, with roughened edges, that interlocked in an elaborate framework system like a LEGO set. "Great stuff," said the wall builder. "Easy to use. It'll never fall down. They use it for highways." My heart sank, but, determined to save money for the rest of the garden—the stuff was affordable—I picked the most rustic-looking molded stone I could find. My intention was to cover the wall with plants as quickly as possible, and I hoped that it would not have the same repulsiveness quotient that the old one had had.

Leonard's friend the wall builder had, coincidentally, done all the drainage work uphill from my yard, as well as all the excavation, for my new neighbors in the Victorian house, the ones who owned the stone carriage house. Perhaps not so coincidentally. The neighbors had given me his name, too, when I had gone to inquire about who was responsible for the collapsed concrete; the wall builder had been the one blasting and drilling, grinding the gears, pushing around the mountains of earth. He had routed all the water running off their yard into a narrow trench behind the concrete wall, which was supposed to drain onto my driveway through a clay pipe that was a hundred years old.

The wall builder, as laconic a fellow as ever there was, summed up my problem nicely: "I guess your yard became their dry well."

No old wall could have withstood the pressure of so many tons of water suddenly barreling down behind it. Nevertheless, the collapse of my simple concrete slab came as a surprise.

I ventured, with naive fury, into my first entanglement over property rights. It had been established, by the neighbors' surveyor, that the concrete wall holding up their garage was on my land, and belonged to me. (In all those years I had never had the property lines staked out; why would I? Note to all homeowners: have a clear idea of the boundaries of your garden the moment you buy your house, if not before.) The neighbors, when I went to talk to them, pleasantly jettisoned any responsibility for what, after all, looked like an act of God. Who could have forseen such a calamity? Perhaps the wall had simply grown weary. The truth of what had happened was as murky as the water that had poured into my garden.

My neighbors were lovely people, and they told me they had renovated the carriage house so their children's grandmother, a retired schoolteacher whose debilitating illness had confined her to a wheelchair, could come for lengthy visits. How the children loved sitting in her cozy, tiny house, and how she loved children. How she had decorated the walls so sweetly. How much easier it was for her to spend evenings in the carriage house, rather than drive back and forth to New Jersey. How wonderful for the children to get to know their grandmother. The blasting of stone had happened to remove obstacles and more easily link the carriage and the main houses. Then came the laying out of wider, paved paths to accommodate Grandmother's wheelchair, the new gutters to reroute the rain that was rotting her roof. All this work had set into motion the drainage work. The neighbors were not, of course, saying that the drainage work had caused the retaining wall to fall. That was unfortunate.

Upon hearing of the adored grandmother confined to her wheelchair, her grandchildren at her knees in the carriage house, my stiff resolve to take a stand crumpled immediately.

The neighbors offered to pay for a new pipe that would carry water past the back of my yard, a piece of plastic which was, in the end, a bargain. I was left to pick up the cost of digging new drains, deciding about dry wells (real ones), figuring out what to do about a driveway now so deeply eroded that you could actually fall into it (and many did—the Boys had begun a vigorous Campaign for Driveway Reform)—all this expense, to say nothing of building a new wall.

The building of the new wall was to have a domino effect. Somehow, when the wall fell down, it took with it all the resistance I had been stockpiling, over so many years, to putting my own large imprint on the rest of the garden. In crushing the very little I had added to my yard—the postage stamp of the Back Bed—the wall forced me to make some major decisions. It was time for a commitment to the rest of the yard. Either that, or time to give up, call it quits, and find a new home. That was out of the question. With the wall down, and the Back Bed gone, a newly opened area would provide the only access to the side of the yard, the only way to truck in a significant amount of trees and shrubs and soil and whatever else I would want. It was the classic window of opportunity—even I could see that. It was time to recapture what I had sarcastically, during years of neglect, referred to as the Back Forty (even though it was really the side yard; I liked the implication that that part of the property was too far from my thoughts to do much about it, even though I thought about it all the time). It was time to build a New Back Bed, time to connect the various parts of the garden and give the whole thing a more rigorous design. It was time to reclaim my property, and create for myself all the little crannies of a garden that give such pleasure, in which to wander, or sit and rest. It was time to pay the Helpful Men to come to my rescue.

For years, I had thought that I had been unable to remake the garden out of intimidation, ignorance, sadness, lassitude, and lack of imagination. The summer after the wall fell down, I realized that all those reasons were compelling, but another was the most important: I had simply not been ready. The small marks I had made on my patch of earth up until then had been heartfelt but tentative, inquiries into possibility—leaving plenty of room to back off. All the years of doodling and dreaming had been necessary. And therein slipped one of those life lessons you are lucky to notice. It can certainly take a long time to know what you want. You cannot force yourself to the understanding. But there are times when you cannot really know what you can—or should—do until you begin to act. And it was only when I started to transform my own garden that I truly understood what it meant to be a suburban gardener in the twenty-first century.

The morning the wall fell, it was as if a dam had burst. My grief at all that I had lost, pent up behind my own walls of silence and inactivity, was finally washed away. I had needed the release. Another wall was eventually built. It was ungainly, just like the old wall, but in a new way. I was afraid it was the sort of thing the True Love would sniff at, but that gave me a curiously perverse pleasure—as if that indicated that I was released from his spell, too. The new wall was solid; it would last my lifetime, said the proud wall builder. And, the most important thing of all: it would handle trouble. I could learn a few things from this wall. It could withstand pressure. It had proper drainage.

For it turns out, surprisingly enough, that what is most essential to the strength of a wall is a proper weep hole.

# FOUR

# THE LITTLE WHITE BIRD

*"Every landscape is, as it were, a state of the soul, and whoever penetrates into both is astonished to find how much likeness there is in each detail."*

—Henri Frédéric Amiel

A few weeks after the wall fell, it was raining again, and as I made another morning's cup of coffee, I noticed a puddle on the floor where one should not have been. (Of course there are always the usual puddles, around plants you have watered, for instance, or the dishwasher.) There was no mistaking this puddle, though. It was a problem. It was raining into the house.

Another sign?

First the retaining wall, now the roof. Bad omens again?

Water everywhere; so many problems with water. I wanted to blame everything on the True Love; after all, he made me cry. My troubles were beginning to seem alarmingly related. Surely it was a sign, at least to call the roofer. He arrived promptly, inspired by emergency, splashed a black patch of tar onto the roof to stop the leak, and said he would return the next day to investigate the source of the problem. The next day came, and the next day went. Over the next few weeks I begged, whined, and wheedled, which is what you have to do to make men come back when they said they would, and you don't want to sound too bossy or uppity (in which case they will never return). The roofer promised to make some time on his calendar to reroof all the porches. There are four of them. Definitely this was a sign of impending financial distress.

The roofer eventually stopped returning my calls altogether. Just as I was beginning to think that any ambitious plans for the garden would have to be shelved because there would soon be nothing left of the house, Leonard, having introduced me to the wall man, came around again to talk garden business. I had not thought to call Leonard for help with the roofer, but he immediately demonstrated a valuable lesson about Helpful Men: they are in league, the Helpful Men. They prefer to talk only to one another. They respond to one another. As one explained it, the pitch of a woman's voice is almost impossible for them to hear, as it is out of their aural range. All they want from you is to be paid. Also, it is through their cell phones that Helpful Men are most vulnerable. Want the Helpful Man? Get the cell phone number (not so easy as you might think; they are closely guarded). Leonard got the roofer on his cell phone then and there, and told him he couldn't begin to think about putting in the garden until he had finished his roofing job; it was unthinkable to work with all the debris flying around, so the roofer's delay was costing him, Leonard, some serious business. Leonard was effective. The roofer set a date to begin the job.

That settled, we turned to the garden. Leonard was an amiable sort of person. He seemed to understand, as only a gardener could, that I was on the edge of hysteria at the loss of so much of the Back Bed. He made sympathetic clucking noises. It was a shame I had waited so long to call and so many plants had spent weeks under a concrete slab. Still, he had hope. He would save what he could, and we would replant the rest.

"While we're at it," I began—and soon enough I was walking him around the garden, telling him my fantasies about the Back Forty, with its dead and dying hemlocks, its forlorn patches of grass, blanketed in too deep a shade under a neighbor's messy Norway maple—a tree that had given me fits for years. We stood and talked under the canopy of my favorite tree, a regal, hundred-and-fifty-year-old oak, and I made a special point about how I wanted to be careful with three old and slightly cranky dogwood trees.

We walked the length of the Back Forty—I wanted Leonard to feel the promise of that space—over to the far side of the yard and stood at the chain-link fence that separated me from a neighbor's house. This was the part in which the hemlocks had been planted at least fifty years ago, judging by their size, to screen out that house. Propped up against the rusting, curling fence on the neighbor's side (and who did that fence belong to? I wondered—and did not want to know) were several large, bald black tires, what looked like a dead battery, and a crumpled and rusted garbage can. They had become permanent fixtures in my landscape. The fence was clogged with honeysuckle and poison ivy, but naturally nothing grew near the toxic rubber of the tires. It was obvious that we needed a new screen between our houses; the one time I had telephoned the neighbor to ask if he would remove the junk from view, he hung up on me. Leonard laughed when I pointed out an ancient, rusting VW bus permanently parked at the top of the driveway. On its roof lay a thick mulch of pine needles; gaily patterned curtains hung in the windows. The rumor among the children in the neighborhood was that there was a dead body in the bus; the dare was to get close enough to peer in through the fraying fabric—the skeleton was said by some to be sitting up at the wheel.

"Oh, yeah, I know that guy," Leonard said. "A real character. A musician. He is living with his aging mother."

(There was a time when most of the houses on my block seemed to be occupied by men who had left their wives and children and come back to their own childhood homes to live once again with their mothers or fathers. For many years four grown boys in their forties and fifties lived in the house next door on the opposite side of the VW bus, with their father and sixty or seventy mounted animal heads, trophies of a lifetime of big game hunting. The animals, elaborately horned and striped, would peer out the window, their glassy eyes catching the late-afternoon light, startling passersby. Every afternoon the father would wander, in his slightly addled fashion, a couple of blocks to the local drugstore and fill his pockets with candy, then come back and sit placidly on the bench by my kitchen door waiting for me to come home, one of my sons clinging to his neck and the other cradled in his lap, the older one smashing chocolate into his mouth as fast as he could, the baby clenching his melting, lumpy sweets in his chubby fists. Eventually, the house, like so many others, went on the market to be bought by a new generation of families, like mine. Prospective buyers reported seeing cages in the basement in which large monkeys were said to have been left.)

Leonard could sense immediately that I was one of those slow, deliberate customers who needed to take her time getting started on things; daydreaming, planning, talking, changing my mind, all very time-consuming. I had had only fifteen years to think about what to do. Probably he could also figure out that I was a slowpoke from the fact that most of the stuff in the side yard was old—mature would be too polite a description—dead or dying. Even while we strolled the yard, I began to dawdle over exactly how big was the scope of this project, backtracking. Maybe I wasn't so sure I would tackle the entire garden this year. Maybe next spring. Maybe in a decade. Maybe it was enough just to get a new wall built.

It was overwhelming, he had to agree. And why bother? I went on, aloud. Just so another wall could fall down? I suddenly felt defeated. Leonard watched my mood slip.

"So," Leonard said, looking at his watch, closing up his clipboard, putting away his pen. "I don't know when I can get started. I'm really busy. Totally backed up. I have no time to fish. And I love to fish. Business is incredible! Incredible! Don't tell me about the economy."

Reverse psychology. I could smell it a mile away. After all, it often worked its magic on my children. And now I was falling under its spell.

"But I don't know," said Leonard. "I don't want a big business. I want a small business. A business I can handle by myself, since I can't find anyone to help me. How do you find all those incredibly helpful people you work with? They are so nice, when I can't get you on the phone. I can't handle how busy I am. So backed up—"

"No, Leonard. No. You don't understand. We have to

get going immediately. You have to bump me up in your calendar."

"I don't know, I don't know. I am already so backed up—"

"Please. I beg you. I am one of your oldest customers. I've lived here forever. I send my friends to shop at your place. I was buying plants from you fifteen years ago. Those are *your* plants under that concrete. Your grandfather worked on this place. You just said so. We don't have to finish fast. We just have to start fast. This is going to be big, Leonard. This is going to be a big project. I mean, not too big. Not too big for you," I said, catching myself.

If he was using reverse psychology on me—effectively, I might add—I was using plain, old-fashioned wheedling on him.

"Please. I beg you. Just squeeze me in."

"Well . . . But I have to tell you, I'm not going to draw up plans, or any of that fancy stuff. You look like the kind of person who wants pretty pictures. *Drawings,*" he said, stretching it out with contempt. "How this is going to look, where that will go. I have to warn you, I'm not going to give you pretty pictures. It never works. Women get disappointed. A plant list, fine. An estimate, even—"

"Gee, thanks—"

"But a watercolor? No. No plans. I don't do plans."

"Fine. No plans. No pretty pictures. No drawings." I was happy to buy a little more time to remain uncommitted to how the garden would look, myself. I didn't want his pictures. I wanted my own.

"Okeydokey, then. I'll be here next week, with my men."

It was time to get to work. Time to stop the deep-breathing exercises, and time to practice detachment from worldly possessions, at least those residing in my bank account.

Soon, my place was crawling with Helpful Men, an unusual situation. Naturally, the roofer, as soon as he began his work, found termites—he came to my door triumphantly bearing an armful of blackened, shredded, and munched wood and a clear plastic baggie swarming with bugs, nasty-looking things, flicking their wings angrily in their ballooning trap. The front porch turned out to be so rotten it was about to fall off. (I had seen those bugs swarming around the roof columns, looking strangely like flying ants, and knowing nothing about bugs, I had supposed they were misguidedly looking for flowers among the gigantic stalks of porch columns; I assumed bugs only wanted to be outside, where they belonged, and not inside.) Naturally, we disturbed an entire family of skunks underneath another rotten porch. Naturally, the wall builder misunderstood my directions and built the wall too short by ten feet. Naturally, that was my fault. Naturally, once the concrete slab was bulldozed off the bed, Leonard could save nothing.

"But that's okay. I've got plenty of stuff at the nursery. Too much stuff. I don't have enough time to fish."

I felt like locking the door and abandoning the house and garden to the rains and the pests. I offered the roofer my keys.

"I give up," I said one morning. "Take them. I'm going to work. Just tell the Boys, when they come home from school today, to find another place to live. I am leaving."

The roofer was such a capable person that he only chuckled and shook his head.

"Don't worry." And then the mantra. "Everything will be fine."

"Can you fix everything?" I was whining plaintively by then. "Can you put everything back together again?" It seemed inconceivable.

"Impossible," he said. And then laughed at the impact of his clever joke. "Anything can be fixed, honey. Just not the crack of dawn. Or a broken heart. Everything else just takes time and money. I have the time. You have the money. We're perfect together. Don't worry."

I was consoled. I like a straightforward relationship. Soon, new studs were being hammered into place, and new porches were going up. The new wall was built. And dismantled. And rebuilt. While they were at it, the carpenters built a bookcase in the laundry room to contain the spillover of books from the kitchen, as well as the vases I was unable to stop buying. The men were indeed helpful. But was it necessary to rip that branch off the old yew simply because it got in the way of the porch railings? Was it necessary to leave the yard strewn with curls of copper scraps and daggerlike splinters of cedar? Was it necessary to drop a hammer down the chimney? Yes. Necessary, and inevitable. Helpful Men do not think trees feel anything, or care if they do. And they do not clean up.

As the summer reached its peak, Leonard and I began a series of discussions about how to redesign the Back Forty, the side garden; I should more properly call it the side yard, for there really was no garden left in it, and barely any landscaping worth the name, for that matter. The last of the dying hemlocks would be removed; they were no longer screening anything. Only one of the more than twenty that had been standing when we had moved in fifteen years earlier seemed to have remained healthy. The younger trees that a friend and I had planted a couple of years earlier would need rearranging and transplanting. The dogwoods looked healthy, just a few thin spots in their limbs, and there were puddles of pachysandra thriving underneath them. (It is fashionable these days to disdain pachysandra but I found it to be a durable and thick ground cover, and I liked its understated stalks of white flowers in the spring. It seems fashionable, I notice, to be disdainful of most of the things that are typical of a suburban garden, the things that were so abundantly planted in the fifties—azalea, vinca, pachysandra, rhododendron, forsythia. Now there is even a campaign of disdain for daffodils. But these plants are thriving for a reason. They do well in suburban conditions, with inexpert gardeners. I find plant snobberies to be misguided and useless. Except for mine. Take baby's breath, for instance: *Gypsophila paniculata*. Why would anyone want to plant something that looked like droplets of sputum that had been sneezed onto the ground?)

I did not want to make room for more lawn in the side yard, as what was there was struggling in the shade of the rocky soil. In fact, I had fired the mowers earlier that summer, because they seemed to be mowing everything in their paths and overcharging for what little mowing really needed to be done.

I wanted a new garden that I could maintain by myself, as I had never had any help taking care of it before (apart from mowing). And I did not expect to have flowers in the side yard; once new trees went in to replace the dead ones—and under the canopy of the neighbor's maple—there would not be enough sun for perennials. I had learned that much.

The sunny Back Bed, once it was rescued from the concrete slab, small though it was, would have held plenty of flowers for me, had I had the brains to replant it with flowers. As the new wall was going up, Leonard and I had agreed to fill the New Back Bed first, so that by the next spring, when I would start planting out the Back Forty, there would be something green and inspiring to look at in the new beds. That was when I made my first big mistake. Thinking only of the crushing loss of the old bed, I replanted everything the way it used to be. I should have known better than to proceed in such a piecemeal fashion, and worse, to try to recapture the past.

Over the years, my sunny Back Bed had become a semi-shaded bed, as the shrubs I had planted had grown to ten or fifteen feet. The perennials I had put in had straggled out miserably from under the shade of the shrubs, and I had begun replacing them with ferns and hosta whose leaves were the size of dinner plates. By the time the wall fell, my Back Bed was an eccentric mix of shade- and sun-loving plants. The second time around, I put in a new row of rose of Sharon, but alternated it with another shrub, the Chinese snowball (*Viburnum macrocephalum*), for I loved its brilliant pom-poms of flowers. Apart from the fact that I had not chosen the right plant, as I had meant to select the fragrant *V. carlcephalum,* I didn't think about how the viburnum would look in the hot sun, during the rest of the summer, when it had passed its bloom. Its leathery leaves got burnt and crispy, and no amount of watering helped. The hydrangeas that I had planted in the bed fifteen years earlier had been standardized, trained to grow on a single stem. They had repeatedly strangled themselves; they would thrive for two or three years, and suddenly collapse. When I dug them out, I found that their roots had wrapped themselves around the stems, and as they grew larger the roots grew tighter, and eventually the plant choked itself. I was sure the standardization had something to do with the unbearable torque on the plant, and it was because of the hydrangeas that I have never again used standardized plants in my garden. They are too prissy. I like shrubs that have at least two feet planted solidly in the ground.

However, I decided not to plant any hydrangeas, in shrub form, in the New Back Bed; there was a hydrangea being trained to creep over the wall. I had room for three rose of

Sharon and two viburnums, each plant about fifteen to twenty-five inches tall. I planted at their feet hosta, fern, and other shade-loving plants, because hosta and fern had been growing in the crushed bed. In other words, I planted a shade garden, in full sun, to replace what had only become a shade garden after fifteen years. All because I wanted things to be exactly the way they once were, I ignored the nature of what I had been given at that moment: a brilliantly sunny spot, and the only sunny spot in my entire yard. I also ignored Leonard.

(I only understood how wrong I had been late the next spring, nearly a year later, when I was finished with planting the rest of the garden and, coming full circle, saw that the New Back Bed was languishing and would not do at all. The only thing that seemed happy was the clinging hydrangea that was creeping up the wall—my first priority, having built a new wall, was to cover it up as fast as I could. Probably the weep holes helped the vine get enough moisture in that sunny spot. What an ill-conceived bed. But I took some comfort in the idea that even misguidedly replacing the old bed had gotten me started on replanting the entire garden. Within weeks of realizing my mistake, I found myself happily doing exactly what I had done sixteen years earlier: jamming into the New Back Bed those sun-loving perennials, lilies and fairy roses and lavender and all manner of beauties in great profusion.)

Leonard and I had begun to rough out a design for the Back Forty. We could do nothing to put it into place; I had dragged my feet such a long time, in the planning process, that autumn was drawing to a close, and the nursery was short on supplies. My plan was to continue dreaming about the side yard through the winter with a firm resolve—and a promise from Leonard to return—to hit the ground early in the spring. And so I embarked on the Winter of Last Daydreams; it was to be a fertile period, though the ground outside remained frozen for a long time.

Leonard and I were walking through the yard early one morning at the beginning of winter, reviewing the possibilities ahead one last time before the cold settled in seriously. His crew had delivered enough firewood to see me through the Ice Age. I was (of course) adding to our book-length list of what would go where, haggling over what to keep, what to transplant. We had started laying out the outlines of the new beds with colorful cords I had bought at the hardware store. With every walk-through, the shapes of the beds changed, but I knew I had the Winter of Last Daydreams ahead of me to mull it all over. Leonard was fun to talk to. He was entering a boyish middle-age; he was overstressed; and, as he constantly told me, the demands of the business were taking a toll on his wife, and on his heart. (Why do men worry so about their hearts? They all do, even twelve-year-old men—their hearts and their knees.)

Our walkabouts were extremely productive. "I should just sell the business. But I love the business. It's a family business. What do you think of some more laurel in this corner?"

On we went, in that vein. "Not enough time for fishing, how about more rhododendron? Not enough good gardeners to hire, I can't find anyone to help me in the nursery, it's really tough, what would you think of moving that *Cedrus atlantica*? My kids don't seem interested in the business, how about hosta everywhere? But they're young, I guess; you're right. Maybe after they start kindergarten. No, no hosta there. You want more ferns?"

Suddenly I noticed, at the corner of my house next to the living room, a flash of light on the ground under a large old yew tree. We walked closer, and, pushing aside some branches, we ducked under to peer at the apparition. It was a perfect ring, about two feet in diameter, of pure, white feathers. It was uncanny, how symmetrically, how meticulously, the circle was laid out. It was beautiful, and terrible.

"Uh-oh," said Leonard, glancing around uneasily. "Looks like a cat got something." It is a fact that the neighborhood cats hung around my garden, known to them, no doubt, as the Happy Hunting Grounds. I often left teacups of milk out on the stoop for the innumerable stray kittens that came my way. The True Love (completely lost, it seemed clear, by that winter, as I had still not seen or heard from him for many long months) had been a fine one for putting strange things in the ground, leaving his mark on my territory, I suppose. It had been because of the True Love (perhaps not so true) that I had had new insight into the nature of my dream garden; he actually enjoyed sitting in the yard, and that gave me hope for its appeal. He had arrived one day bearing pots full of *Nepeta cataria,* or catnip. That was an extra draw for the mewling citizenry; the True Love planted the herb, which immediately took root and began to spread wildly. The Boys and I were delighted to watch the cats nibble and roll and purr languorously in the fragrant patches, then walk daintily but crookedly away, dopily, happily, stoned.

Cats will be cats, I thought, poking at the white ring, but I felt bad for this poor bird. Peering closer, I noticed that there were no bones visible, only the feathers. I comforted myself, and Leonard, with the fantasy that the bird had only been damaged, and the rest of him had flown away.

"What could have been such a pure white?" I wondered aloud. Leonard shrugged helpfully. "A dove? Maybe a chicken?"

We left that mandala in the dirt, and strolled into the far end of the side yard to check on the status of the neighbor's dead batteries, chatting about trout streams and more hydrangea. I had taken a particular liking to *Hydrangea quercifolia,* an oak-leaf variety with big, handsome panicles of white flowers that I had seen thriving in Central Park. We walked to the neighbor's chain-link fence—more cars had appeared in the drive in the last month—and, turning to survey my house, I saw on the ground next to me a fresh heap of ripped white feathers, larger even than the first batch. It was the rest of the bird. I could see a bit of backbone, a shred of flesh hanging off it, and one pink claw, large, dagger sharp, and pearly toed.

"Mind if I examine this? You gonna faint?" Leonard picked it up.

"I'm fine," I replied, never one to let a man best me on nerve. "Let me see."

There was a thin metal bracelet around the rough hosiery of the leg. Could it have been an escaped chicken? But the foot looked too dainty, almost regal, the toes manicured, not the sort of foot that spent its days scratching for food in the dirt. I fiddled with the band and saw it was inscribed with a message—*Abe's TNT Fliers*—and a phone number. I copied it down.

"What do you think, Leonard?" I said. "Is it a sign?"

"A sign?"

"Yeah. You know. An omen. Is it a bad sign? A good one?"

Leonard looked at me with pity and sweetness. "It's a good sign." He might as well have added, *There, there, dear.*

I brightened at his confident tone. Here was a guy who understood things. "Really? What does it mean?"

"It means someone had a good breakfast in your garden. It isn't a good sign. It isn't a bad sign. It's just a sign that something happened."

Leonard went back to his stressful job, and I went inside and dialed the number on the band. Abe answered on the first ring, and I imagined him anxiously sitting by the phone, waiting for word about a bird that did not come home last night. I asked him where I was calling. Near the Bronx Zoo, he said; that is, just a few miles from my house.

"Well, Abe," I said, trying to think how to be gentle about this difficult talk. "I have good news and bad news. The good news is I found your bird. The bad news is, there isn't much left of it. Something ate it."

Silence.

"What was it, Abe?"

Abe was implausibly cheerful, I thought. "Probably one of my homing pigeons. I got dozens. I raise them on the roof. Sounds like a hawk got it. Happening more and more these days. I train those birds to race and carry messages."

Messages? So there. It *was* a sign.

"There's a whole website on homing pigeons; you should check it out. There's tons to learn about them. I was in Connecticut this week; they had a bird fair, and the birds there, they had some nice ones, they're selling for a hundred bucks apiece. Real beauties. Amazing. You should check it out. If you're interested. It's wwwpigeonworld.com. I think. Maybe not. Who can remember all this crap?"

"But the hawks, Abe. What about the hawks?"

I am passionate about hawks; it is something of a joke with the Boys, how I see hawks everywhere, no matter where we are. "Look, Mom!" one of them will say, pointing vaguely at a squirrel, or a pigeon, or a pay phone, or a traffic light. "Look! Stop the car! A hawk!"

The Boys can laugh all they want. The hawks are always around me, wheeling over the station while I wait for my train in the morning, sitting on top of my garage. (Did hawks eat kittens? Was I baiting them for a terrible end with those teacups of milk on my kitchen stoop?)

"The hawks, they got nowhere to go anymore. So much building going on everywhere. There's no more country left. So they come to the Bronx. They see plenty of garbage. They see plenty of rats. They see their kind of fast food. They see my beautiful pigeons, all white and perfect; they look good to them. The hawks want to race them. Sometimes they win. Not always. They win, the hawks eat my birds. It's only natural."

Between the floods and the termites and the hawks, to say nothing of the True Love's peregrinations, too many natural things had been happening that year. It was all a bit ominous. For days I went around asking people what the death in my garden of the little white bird could mean. I knew it was a sign, but of what? It is astonishing how the subject of reading signs clams people up. Finally I found someone able to venture a cogent theory: the little white bird butchered in my garden, he said, meant that it was time to let go of a troublesome person. If I was thinking about getting rid of someone, now was the time to do it. I should proceed, he said.

"Someone troubling you at the office?" my friend inquired gravely.

"No. Someone has been troubling my sleep," I said, thinking of the wayward True Love. "But that is over. He is out of my life. This time for good. I got the message. At least the bird didn't lose his life for nothing."

And a wall falling down, well, that is a good sign, my friend said, a sign that you are ready to move on. Of course you must rebuild the wall, he went on, because it serves a useful purpose. But you will build a better, stronger wall, more secure, and it will be a wall you know through and through, what's in front, what's behind.

Of course.

And on the verge of my karmic breakthrough, who should reappear but the True Love. Several weeks after the incident with the hawk and the white bird (several months after I had "moved on" from said troublesome person), the True Love invited me to a holiday lunch, as Christmas was upon us. An olive branch was extended. We would settle into a new friendship. Grievances would be forgotten. This time everything would go smoothly. I knew my limits. More important, I knew his. And so did he. Well, there is nothing like the True Love to rekindle hope, to say nothing of delusion.

I was delighted at the prospect of seeing him, eager to tell him about my plans for the garden. He had actually been the first person—the first man—to give me a hand (free of charge, no grumbling) in the garden. The True Love had heard nothing about the arrival of Helpful Men in my life; I knew he would appreciate them. He did not know that the wall had fallen, and that my garden had lain for months in ruins, that I was defeated, but that I was not going to remain defeated—either by him or by my garden—and that I had entered the misty realms of a Winter of Last Daydreams, and planned to emerge prepared to tackle the rest of the yard. I was curious about what he would have to say about my schemes for redesigning the Back Forty. He was the *only* person in weeks with whom I had not discussed my garden; I knew it was tiresome and I was happy to have a new audience. The True Love had certainly heard enough of my idle fantasies about What I Would Do If I Had Time / Money / Energy / Hope / Etc. (You supply your own ending. This is a useful lament and should be hauled out frequently. By now you can see that whenever you think you are contemplating your garden, you are really—as you cut across the lawn and trail along the flower beds and duck through the hedge to find a quiet place in the shade—thinking about love, and despair, and safety, and hope.)

Of course the True Love had heard nothing about the hawk and its breakfast of the little white bird, and I particularly looked forward to telling him about that, as he was amusingly squeamish. "The amorality of nature," he would say indignantly, his eyebrows rising in alarm, his mouth puckering in dismay—plus he could wriggle his scalp from ear to ear on command—when hearing about a cat mauling a mouse, or an osprey twisting the head off a fish, as if such behavior were shocking, and a grave disappointment to him, personally.

When I got to the restaurant—a posh place where we loved to have lunch because it felt like being in someone's Parisian dining room (plus it had an endlessly intriguing wine list)—and sat down at the table, I noticed gifts all around my plate, gaily wrapped in colored paper, gold, green, red, that glittered in the otherwise restrained atmosphere. I laughed with delight. Heads began to turn. In my water glass was a scroll, tied with a trailing blue ribbon, on which was printed an index to the gifts, as well as instructions for the order of opening. Laughter and applause moments were carefully indicated. Well, you couldn't say you didn't know where you were, with the True Love. He gave you a script. When I lifted my napkin to place it in my lap, I discovered a gift hidden under the linen. Such was his boyish, jolly charm. Even the dignified waiter was amused, and permitted a smile to hover across his face. The True Love's blue eyes twinkled merrily, his suit rumpled cheerfully; only his elegant silvery tie maintained the proper decorum. He could barely contain a gleeful crow at his clever and wily ways. What a wonderful surprise. What a seduction. I was a goner. Again.

I unwrapped a beautiful old book, a first edition by one of my favorite authors, J. M. Barrie, the man who had written the beloved *Peter Pan*. It was in the book I had just been given, written before the chronicles of Wendy, Tinkerbell, and Captain Hook, that the character of Peter Pan had first appeared, a newly hatched Lost Boy who could still feel the itchy place between his shoulders where his wings had once been.

The book was called *The Little White Bird*.

# SITTING AROUND

*"From perplexity grows insight."*
—Karl Jaspers
*The Great Philosophers*

I had been dragging lawn chairs all over my yard for years, since the day I had moved in and first taken a rest in the garden, trying out pools of sun or shade, contemplating the view of the house from one and then another angle through the trees, or across the tattered ribbon of a lawn. I was often drawn to a corner deep in the Back Forty, one that had nothing in particular to recommend it, save for the dwindling shelter of a few dying hemlocks, and its ample remove from the house. What I loved about that far corner was the long view over the yard and to the house. It was a deeply satisfying perspective. The chair in that far corner gave me some distance on the house; sitting there in the twilight, contemplating my dreams for the garden that I would one day plant, gazing into the living room through the old French doors, I felt simultaneous and conflicting waves of proud possessiveness and disassociation. There is a fascination in looking into your own house as if you were a stranger, especially at the gloaming of the day, when the rooms are lit up, and everyone inside is going about their business as if they were on a stage, but not knowing that they are being watched, one son practicing the piano, which he is supposed to be doing, the other tossing a ball around in the living room, which he is decidedly not supposed to be doing. I would gaze into my house, and wonder what I was looking for, and wonder at where life had taken me, and wonder why I was on the outside of my home, and wonder why, over the years, that grew to feel just fine.

That corner was a good place for inspection. I could survey the decline of the hemlocks from that corner, and decide when it was time to take pity and fell another one. I kept a protective eye on the dogwood, my anxiety growing, over the years, as they began to wither and die all over town. I watched the pool of pachysandra under the dogwoods grow wider, its green depths darken with age. From that corner I watched a small, accidental bed behind the house, just under the living room window, grow larger and messier; I called it the Holding Pen, because its occupants were the transplants languishing in every other part of the garden. I didn't know what else to do with them but save them until I had figured out the shape of the garden; little did I know that would take more than a decade. It was from that corner that I watched with spreading concern as one uphill neighbor's Norway maple grew unchecked, at an alarmingly rapid clip, larger and more dense, unkempt, shading out the little bit of grass in my yard, and the privet hedge in his, until large clumps of it were no more than dead sticks upright in a dusty soil; that hedge was meant to afford us both privacy, so that we could sit around in our gardens in solitude. I began to feel exposed, and as the canopy spread, so did my resentment.

I sat around and watched the teak bench I had moved from our last home grow dull and gray and covered with lichen. I had placed that bench on a handsome old slate terrace off to the side of the house; I had never understood why the stone there felt so substantial until Leonard pointed out admiringly, one day, that the edge of each piece had been hand-hewn and chiseled into position. Today stone is cut by machine; the sharp, clean edges rob from it the subtle visual cues that give a sense of the weightiness of each slab. I made arrangements of potted plants on the side terrace, and studied the compositions from my chair in the corner, getting up to rearrange the pots to greater effect, and sinking back down again. I could take in the porch that ran across the side of the house; it had been enclosed when we arrived, its thick columns encased in the walls of what had been meant as a solarium, but never quite made it. Curiously, the previous occupants had built a grill in that room, but had neglected to vent it to the outside, causing such a smoky disaster the first time I lit a fire that it was at that moment I decided to tear down the walls and return the room to the porch it had been meant to be. The porch immediately became my summer living room.

It was from the corner seat that, one year, I noticed the wisteria climbing pell-mell across the roof and onto the chimney; it was from that corner I saw the gutter dangling off the front of the house; it was from that corner, one evening in a summer twilight when all the shading leaches out of the day's colors and only the contrasts stand out, that I first understood that the hard white paint of the trim was wrong for the house; the dark cedar shingles disappeared with dusk, leaving the trim outlined against the screen of sassafras in front, and the effect was that of a child's drawing. Months later, from that chair, dragged from one part of the yard to another, I decided that the house needed a dark, green-black paint on the trim that would blend with the shingles and meld into the woods in front. From where I sat, the result of the paint job gave the house an understated elegance. (From where he sat, my father, visiting one day, declared the whole effect "lugubrious.")

We spend so much time inside our houses, looking out, and not enough time looking at our houses from the outside. They are altogether different creatures from that perspective. There were many corners, in the garden, from which to contemplate the big picture.

As the Winter of Last Daydreams began, I suddenly realized what I had been doing, all those years, dragging furniture around the yard. I had been conjuring up the contours of my idealized garden.

Landscape designers sometimes talk about "desire paths": the paths traced by people's habits of movement from one place to another, the paths that make clear where we want to go, and how we want to get there. Regardless of the paths laid down by the professionals who have designed a park, say, or a public garden, people will cut their own convenient, or pleasurable, ways through yards and meadows and fields, leaving behind trampled grass or dirt footpaths that indicate the route they insist on taking. The professional designer, setting out to reorganize a landscape, ignores these markers at his peril. You can see paths of desire everywhere: slicing across the grassy median strips in parking lots; traversing playing fields; wending through city parks. Our own foot-steps etch our desires into the ground. Just before the end of my suburban street the commuters have veered off the side-walk to head uphill across a grassy strip of land to get to the train station—every second counts, at rush hour; this scramble has gone on for so many years that the town finally succumbed and paved the walkway for us. (Even something that seems as rooted as a tree cuts its own path of desire; I have come to know several quite well on my way to the station, and have watched over the years as the roots of the solitary tulip tree, an oak, and the ancient sugar maple on the next block have hurled themselves up over the confines of a concrete edge and into a nearby patch of soil to find sustenance.) And of course animals cut very clear paths to their feeding troughs, or their watering holes, or their nests; deer in winter will always cross a field in a file, leaving a surprisingly narrow, delicate trace in the snow; skunks leave in your lawn their paths of desire with their fossicking noses.

We create paths of desire in so many ways, not just with our feet; our daily rituals leave behind poignant reminders of our little ways. The candle that burns through the evening and drips through the slatted dinner table, leaving a path of waxy mounds on the bluestone, as the table is moved to catch the last rays of the summer light. The greasy arc of spots on the stone where the scraps of meat are dropped for the stray cat who always knows when to appear. The matted lawn, because the children will always play catch in a part of the yard where the trees don't get in the way, the sun doesn't get in their eyes. The scraped pad under the favored, dangling seat of the swing set. The cut through the rhododendron by the kitchen door, where the pachysandra is always squashed, because that is the way the Con Ed man has been getting to the meter for years now, and nothing you do, no alternate stepping-stones you place around the shrubbery, will alter his course. His path is straightforward and he has no time to waste. Your garden is full of the souvenirs of living. And, if you take care to find them, it is full of clues that remind you how you have been using it—you have left them there. All gardens contain paths of desire.

As we are not cows, and will probably not do enough heavy foot-dragging in our own pastures to leave behind rutted trails, the furniture we move around the garden becomes an important clue to locating our paths of desire. The far corner, in which I sat hour after hour, was to become an important part of the new garden that I would lay out, though I didn't know it for years.

Quite apart from matters of aesthetics, it is important what kind of furniture you put into the garden, because certain kinds of pieces are liberating, and others are anchoring. You will have to leave off that snobbery about light furniture (of the aluminum and webbing variety), at least while you are in a period of exploration of how to use your garden.

Much as I love teak, I found it impossible to move by myself more than a few inches in any direction. When I started furnishing the house and garden, I went to a tag sale in an old house; everything arrayed on the lawn was from the forties and fifties. I saw some aluminum lawn chairs whose sturdy green webbing was intact. These chairs had been well cared for. My first memory of garden furniture had been of an aluminum lounge chair, a long, low, cotlike affair with the same sort of green webbing. The memory of this chaise was vivid because it also contained the first memory I had of nude sunbathing in the garden. I was probably six or seven years old; I had gone with my mother to visit her friend, Suzanne, who was a very beautiful and thin and childless Frenchwoman. (It fascinates me to realize that both women, so grown-up in my memory, were then much younger than I am now, by at least ten years, just beginning to learn to keep house, to tend their gardens.) I loved visits to Suzanne's house because she was glamorous, and served generous and icy Shirley Temples in tall crystal flutes, no matter what time of day we arrived. Just after breakfast seemed the perfect time for a cocktail. When we couldn't find Suzanne in her house, we went into the garden at the back, yoo-hooing in French for her attention. She called to us from behind a dense circle of tall hedges. Rounding the corner first, I came on to Suzanne stretched facedown across her chaise. She was completely naked. Not in the least bit worried about a bee sting or a mosquito bite on her bare bottom. Her hair was neatly tucked into a white terry-cloth babushka, her toes with their bloodred nails were tucked under the silver bar at the bottom, her hands dangled off the front of the chaise (she was wearing many rings), a white towel was stuffed into the green webbing underneath her glistening, oiled, slightly sweaty skin. There on the ground was a bottle of baby oil—the stuff we used to soften up my little brother! On a grown-up? A silvery sun reflector lay on the grass under her face, and next to it was balanced a tall, thin glass of something refreshing; a cigarette balanced on the edge of an ashtray sent up a thin curl of smoke. Who knew? Did my mother have a naked body, too?

Ever since that fateful day, I have been partial to the liberating promise of lightweight garden furniture. The arms and legs of the chairs at that yard sale had swooping curves; they were wide and comfortable and light. I bought them. Forty bucks for four.

One day, shortly after the announcement of my appointment as the editor of *House & Garden,* I got a call from a friend. He had been at a swanky New York dinner party, and the conversation had turned to media gossip, which then wandered into speculation about how I lived, what my taste was like, and how I would affect the contents of the magazine. One of the guests confessed that, unable to resist her curiosity, she had driven by my house to see what she could see. Not realizing that I had a spy at the dinner table, she went on to mock the lawn furniture she had spotted in the garden. Metal. Plastic. Old. Cheap. A disgrace. And a terrible portent.

This conversation, gleefully reported to me the next day, was disconcerting for any number of reasons—not the least of which is that, in order to see any furniture in my garden, you must travel up the driveway and walk around to the back of the house. Well, I wasn't in too much of a position to protest such a violation of privacy, being the sort of unregenerate snoop who cannot resist the urge to climb a wall to see just what that fragrant blossom is attached to, or tromp through a construction site, or sneak up a driveway ("Come on, don't worry, just go up; if we get caught, we can say we're lost. . . ."). But matters of taste are difficult to articulate, in house or garden design; what is beautiful to your eye may not be appealing to mine. I can learn to understand why you find something handsome—a chair constructed of pressed layers of cardboard; I can educate myself about its design antecedents, or its radical departure from tradition. I can learn to get past an initial discomfort I may feel with the unfamiliar—in a line, an ornamentation, a material. But none of that means that I will ever be able to *feel* the beauty you see—and I cannot be argued into it. So often, our choices have little to do with taste and more to do with necessity— and is that not the famous "function" part of the form and

function equilibrium a good designer seeks? (And, to further complicate things, there is the matter of trends—those
things that last weekend were in people's trash piles are suddenly worth thousands of dollars on the open market. The
trend for stuff from the fifties, like my lawn chair, with its
confident, swooping lines and unabashed celebration of plastic and metal, had, sadly, not arrived in time to rescue my
reputation from the claws at that dinner party.)

The Boys and I happily carried those aluminum chairs all
over the garden: under trees, out into the sunshine, next to the
swing set, over by the sandbox. On cool days I would follow
the patches of sun that would make their way through the
trees; the patches got bigger as more trees came down. In my
chair, in the late-afternoon sun, I was quiet enough to see the
tiny moths and white flies billowing about in circles, going
nowhere, hovering in the last rays of the sun, at the end of their
lives.

Mobility is a must in any garden. You can never get enough
of changing perspective. And as I moved the chairs, I began to
appreciate small things I had not noticed before. I suppose it is
from sitting around that I learned that there is no such thing as
a clean slate upon which to design a garden; there are too
many God-givens, even in a suburban patch that has been
shoved into shape by a bulldozer. When you sit around, you
notice the soil, the path of the sun, the stone outcroppings. The
gentle slope at the side of the yard. The abruptness with which
the stand of sassafras stopped growing, as though someone had
drawn a line of demarcation across the garden many years ago.
The wild daylilies that had sprung up, one summer, of their
own accord, and whose fluorescent pool was growing wider
and wider, spilling down a rocky drop-off in the front of the
yard. The contours of the granite boulders that had been

partly covered over. How far did those shelves of stone extend? I wondered. The protected feeling of sitting under a tree. The warm but exposed feeling of sitting in sunshine.

And, too, over the years of dragging the chairs around, I began to notice how the paint on the sandbox was peeling, how the toys were filthy and half-buried in the sand, how the swing set was falling into disrepair. Much of my yard had long been, rightfully, the domain of the Boys; they were home all day, and played in it, so they made it theirs. A few more years of sitting around went by; I began to notice plastic water guns and small baseball bats abandoned in the pachysandra. I began to accept that my children were exchanging the pleasures of their baby years for other ways to enjoy the garden. That they were growing up, and that the garden would soon swallow up their toys. And as they were getting older, so was the garden, and so was I.

The heavy teak bench in the garden had for years served an entirely different purpose from that of the lightweight chairs that I dragged around. It was in a place where I wanted to stay put. At anchor, so to speak: a heavy bench doesn't move, and neither do you, while you are in it. It invites contemplation; you do not follow the sun, but instead the play of light across the trees, across a patch of grass. You bring cushions, books, teacups or wineglasses, all the sections of the Sunday paper, and a broad-brimmed hat.

That is the part of the garden inviting you to settle down, stay awhile. That is where the True Love sometimes lit up a cigar, and there is nothing nicer than the smell of a good cigar wafting in the fresh evening air—except the smell of a good cigar lingering in a quiet room, around the fireplace, the next morning, especially if someone has left an unfinished glass of fragrant whiskey nearby. By such alchemy, nostalgia is born.

The True Love seemed drawn to the domesticated parts of the garden, those parts with floors. Even though he occasionally looked like a farmer, according to my youngest son, in his flannel shirts and suspendered work pants, he was assuredly a farmer of the gentleman variety. He liked to nibble his way through a dinner outside, and as he was a great appreciator of food, it was fun to watch him eat. He would throw his head back, like a bear, and close his eyes, and wave a piece of pungent cheese back and forth under his flaring nostrils, a smile of rapture spreading across his face. Or he would finger a slab of chocolate, sniffing it, riffling the wrapper, rumbling and growling and purring, nearly licking it before deciding to stick to his diet.

It wasn't just food that I learned to appreciate, sitting around in the garden. It was also the fragrance coming from the flowerpots: the scented geraniums threading their way through a ball of lavender, the aroma of rosemary when I brushed my fingers across the top, the jasmine in flower in August. I would sit, like a dog, nose in the air, parsing out the odors, waiting for a breeze to carry a new perfume past my chair. So many of the white blooms are especially pungent in the evening.

Have you ever noticed how hard it is to sit still in a garden? It is nearly impossible not to let your gaze wander and catch on an errant weed or two; nearly impossible not to get up and start weeding; impossible not to need the clippers to cut down the stray sapling; impossible not to reach into the geraniums and pull out the browned and withered stalks; impossible not to sweep the flagstone; impossible not to rearrange the pots, and then the bench; and then, of course, impossible not to go inside to get more pillows because the bench seems a bit hard, and impossible to sit still on.

But some days I sat, and stayed seated, and that was when I began to notice the undersides of leaves. The tiny stripes under the hemlock needle, when my chair was in their shade. The deep, velvety browns under the rhododendron's leaves, when I sat hidden in the Old Garden; those leaves would curl tightly like cigars when the temperature turned frigid. Part of sitting, of course, involves reading outside; what greater pleasure than being wrapped in a blanket amid pillows with a ray of sunshine falling over a page, as I have done for hours on the teak bench. "My father-in-law (who understood plants) said people go through five stages of gardening," I read one chilly autumn day in a book called *Counting My Chickens,* by the Duchess of Devonshire (it is appropriate to read about royalty when lying around like a princess). "They begin by liking flowers, progress to flowering shrubs, then autumn foliage and berries; next they go for leaves, and finally the underneaths of leaves." I seemed to be in all five stages simultaneously.

It was in a period of unregenerate sitting around that I spent several hours, one morning, by the sunny Back Bed watching a bumblebee play in the pots of jasmine. Four highly articulated legs hugged a tiny white blossom close against its belly, its face pressed to the front of the flower; I watched him insert his head into the tiny, honeyed throat, prising it open farther, slowly, gently, unrelentingly. Soon his fuzzy saffron leggings and long, glistening back were all I could see of the bee. He was buried in the intimate depths of the flower. Before long, white petals were scattered on the flagstone around the pot, the blossoms shredded in the bee's violation. I was spared the arduous task of deadheading the spent jasmine; the bee had done it for me. When the bee emerged I noticed that its wings were frayed, one half torn away; it had been a long summer, so long that the jasmine had flowered four times. The bee dropped heavily to the ground, having penetrated five blossoms, and it lay there awhile, sides heaving, back throbbing. I did not move either.

And, if you sit still, you can watch the driller bees, with their oily bullets of bodies, steadily chew immaculate circular tunnels into your wood furniture, or the eaves of the house, leaving telltale cones of sawdust on the ground below.

From the heavy teak bench I admire my woodpile, a thing that I find extremely satisfying any time of the year. Is it the farmer in me, or the settler? I like the sense of preparedness that a big stack of wood gives, and the memories—and anticipation—of hours by the fire on drafty evenings, which can come at any time of the year. It is worrisome to run low on wood, especially in February, when no one has any left to sell you. This happened to me one winter; I mentioned it to the True Love, how annoying it was to have miscalculated the supplies. The next weekend I nearly fell off the porch tripping over a stack of logs he had cut and split from his own woods, an uncorked bottle of wine, just a glass missing, on top of the pile; the True Love had left the gift sometime earlier in the morning to surprise me.

That bench is in the part of my garden where Bonni (one of the Three Graces, my closest friends) wants to sit and visit, detouring from the train station to my house on those rare evenings when she can unwind from work and escape the chaos at her house to join the chaos at mine (when we are not combining chaotic elements—our children, that is). I take her favorite ashtray out of the cupboard; she settles on the bench and lights up a forbidden cigarette. Whenever Bonni and I sit in the garden, talking and smoking, I feel as though I am a teenager again, about to get caught by the authorities—who in these days happen to be the children, so well indoctrinated in the dangers of cigarettes. Still, heavy benches are there for friends to do as they please.

I nursed my second son, my last baby, sitting on that bench, in that garden. He was old enough, in those warm spring evenings, to pull off my breast, lean away, gaze into my eyes, and give me the benediction of a wide, milk-soaked grin. My breast was like a fountain, started by the strength of his suck and not stopping when he came away, so that milk squirted into his face; I can still see his tiny hand gripping into the side of my breast, hear his gurgling chortle of delight.

Now that baby is old enough to ask me if I will pay him to use stories about him in my books.

One day I came home to find a massive stone table next to the teak bench on the terrace. The previous weekend, I had been sharing the bench with the True Love; we had been reading quietly. I had had nowhere to put down the tea tray—he was sitting on the end that, when I was alone, usually served as a table. He had noticed the awkward arrangement (who wouldn't, as a dessert plate crashed to the ground?). Somehow, he had hauled the surprise around from the driveway to the far side of the garden. It had been carved to look like the pedestal of a column. I didn't know when it had arrived; it turned out I noticed it a couple of days later, and I could not even imagine how the thing had gotten there, it was so heavy. Immovable, I found, when I tried to rearrange the seating. But it began to age quickly, the stone was so porous, and it turned a satisfying mossy yellow-green, and it had a jaunty air. It is good to have a table that won't blow away when you want to picnic in a hurricane.

And from that teak bench I notice that the August garden is the loudest, especially as the sun sets. I wonder, is there a scientific basis for the up tempo of cacophony, the buzzing, the trilling, the vibrato, the sawing, the grinding? What is going on out here? Is everything mating? Or dying? Or both? The cicadas sound like beans, rattled as fast as a hand can shake, in their pods. The cries of children playing in the street are higher-pitched as night falls. The doves moan, and even the cardinals sound frantic; their ritual good-nights are as familiar to me as those I share with the Boys. The cardinals click to one another from deep within the thicket of clematis, the branches of the hemlock, always the same places, year after year.

It is only in a chair, outside, that you can hear the strong voice of the wind whipping through the hemlocks, knocking the swaying sassafras against one another like old bamboo. I like to think that the gusts in spring shake blossoms and leaves loose from limbs, awakening everything.

And of course it is only by sitting around outside that you will think you know what the neighbors are up to, as when I overheard, coming through the straggling privet, the following agonizing exchange:

A man's deep, firm voice: "No. No biting. No biting. No biting. No. No biting allowed."

I heave a sigh, thinking, A new dog. And no fence.

"No. No. No. No. Absolutely no biting."

It is a matter of time before I begin biting.

"But Daddy! I *want* to bite! I *need* to bite!" And a scrawny little voice breaks into a fever pitch of howling.

No dog; that's the good news.

Sitting around: listening, watching, smelling, waiting. Remembering. Learning.

My favorite piece of furniture in the garden is in the halfway zone of the porch—I claim porches as part of the garden, myself. They provide another dimension to it, if you will. I spend many hours sitting on the porches—some of them come off rooms on the second story—gazing at the yard, admiring what is there, imagining what might someday be there. From the porches I can see the patterns of planting quite clearly. I can feel what it is like to be in my trees, rather than underneath them, in particular the dogwoods, whose red, late-summer berries cascade over the layered canopy, and are most visible from above, where the birds find them.

A porch is the only part of the house most clearly seen from the outside, as it is meant to be open to the garden. So a porch ought to be arranged with the garden in mind. I have a large wicker sofa on the one off the living room, with wide, waterproofed cushions. I trained wisteria in a zigzag of lattice up one side of the porch (the only thing the wisteria ever did that was helpful), so that it has made a green curtain, giving the sofa privacy, and I leave a pile of extra cushions by the door that gives onto the porch. What a place to cuddle—and why shouldn't a suburban garden, small and surrounded as it is, have places for naps and kisses?

Now that everything's set up, the porch has become my spring, summer, and autumn living room, so much so that I've added an enormous coffee table for the piles of books and knitting that I take out for the day, for the music player that I hook to an extension cord, for the huge hurricane lamps, for the lunches and dinners that I usually end up eating on the porch. I am so comfortable there, and feel so protected by the thickly woven curtain of wisteria, that I fantasize about finding a couch as big as a bed—one of those opium beds, or the kind of metal beds with three sides that you see in pictures of Provençal gardens—and, dropping the mosquito netting all around my nest, going to sleep for the night out there. With the skunks.

(Which brings up another suburban garden problem: those pesky animals. There is no more beautiful place to be than in a garden at night, but that means the garden should never be illuminated with anything stronger than a candle. Too much lighting, of the sort that climbs up the trees and snakes its way around boulders, is always a terrible idea; it gives your garden a touch of *son et lumière* vulgarity. The visitor expects to pay an admission fee. When you are in the garden at night, you want the caress of moonlight on a white blossom; you want the fine, lacy shadows cast by the flower bed; you want to sniff your way through the dark; you want the black-and-white compositional impact, as you can see no color without light. But candles will not keep away the skunks, who, contrary to their reputations, are not in the least bit shy, or nocturnal. Even floodlights do not have enough wattage to freeze the little criminals in their tracks. So you might as well go to bed indoors and do your strolling by daylight.)

The sofa is the perfect place for early- and late-season catalog reading, and list making; you are near enough to the garden to eye it, from time to time, to see if five hundred more bulbs would fit someplace, and far enough to miscalculate and convince yourself that of course there is room for those bulbs, and why not throw in five new varieties of hosta besides? Oh, the lists of a gardener. They are effusive, energetic, whole-hearted, naïve, sincere, greedy, addled. *I want, I want, I want.* The crossings-out, the adding, the constant, craving desire. The gardener has never enough. I make my lists on stray sheets of paper, and then I throw them away; I should start keeping them in one book, and that way I could look back over years of list making to see if I keep wanting the same things over and over again, and keep talking myself out of them. For years I sat on the sofa and made lists, and dreamed, and doodled, and sketched. For years, I planned for gardens I never planted. I indulged in what I came to think of as a gracious sort of planning: noncommittal, unhurried, evanescent. I felt I could be as delinquent as I wanted about getting out of my chair and following my plans through because I was doing quite enough, simply by sitting around.

The sofa on the porch is also the place to listen to the right kind of rain. There are as many different kinds of rain as there are sunny days; a gardener will never be satisfied to know, simply, that it is raining. There is the hard, fast, driving rain that beats down the flowers (if not the walls) and sluices through the mulch and washes away the topsoil and even rearranges seedlings in their beds. This rain is like a tantrum: violent, and quickly subsiding. The last time we had this kind of rain, which comes frequently in the spring, the dogwood blossoms were flayed off the trees and they lay in tatters all over the grass, like fallen stars, or creatures washed up from the sea. The cherry trees painted the streets pink. There is the light drizzle, the sort that gets your hopes up: *finally, it is raining; I was beginning to think it wouldn't rain anymore.* And then the whole thing is over, and there are dry patches under the trees, even under the slats of the old bench. Simply a light rinse for the leaves. Then there is the perfect rain for the garden, and the best kind to listen to, and as there is very little wind, you are protected under the roof of the porch, behind the curtain of vines; best, your head is resting on the True Love's caged heart, listening to the beats. That heart. Is it too fast? Is it losing beats? Do all men worry about lost beats? The gentle rain will last all day, and with some luck will soak through the mulch, deep into the soil, deeper than your trowel will go, and you will be pleased that everyone has had enough to drink.

The last thing about furniture in the garden: it ought to be used by the gardeners. I am not big on constant industry; or rather, I should say, sitting and thinking are as valuable a sort of industriousness as kneeling and digging. Lolling is important. No one needs to prove, yet again, that a garden is labor intensive, or that our lives progress at a frantic pace. We all know it. It is far more impressive to prove that you are capable of contemplation, that you have learned to safeguard quiet time, that you have developed the concentration to watch a sunflower grow. When your guests arrive in your garden, you should not wait for them to take a seat; you should lead the way to the most comfortable perch. There is nothing worse than having a visit with a gardener who is punching holes in the ground while you are trying to make conversation.

Though I had not left behind traces in the dirt, my furniture-dragging, once I finally started sitting around and thinking, was telling me something about the paths of my heart's desire. That's the best reason I can think of—apart from following the sun through the seasons, or watching for surprising blooms from an innocuous-looking shrub—for delaying awhile, when you move into a house, or while you rest a weary heart, any decisions about what to do with the garden. Where you find yourself sitting will tell you much about the matter of where you will want to be standing on the placement of flower beds, terraces, hedges, heavy benches, trees, and paths. You will spend much time going around in circles, but circling around desire is fruitful. You never know what knowledge you will pick up along the way.

In the Winter of Last Daydreams, my sketches of the garden I wanted began to have a firmer line. I was finally paying attention to my paths of desire, and, along with wishing on a star, that is what you need to start a garden.

# SIX

# THE NEIGHBORS

*"Although affliction cometh not forth of the dust,*
*neither doth trouble spring out of the ground;*
*yet man is born unto trouble,*
*as the sparks fly upward."*

—Job 5: 6–7

I should have known that asking them to cut down the tree was not the right way to begin the conversation. But my hatred of the tree had become desperate, irrational, my mind muddled, my feelings twisted around like the tree's wayward branches. I had to get the question of the maple settled before I planted the new garden; there was one kind of sunshine without it, and much less with it. As the Winter of Last Daydreams spun around, I decided that my neighbors and I needed to have an adult conversation about a problem that had been festering for years. That must have been why I began the discussion with a tantrum.

In every suburban garden, there comes a time to deal with the neighbors. I suppose the reason anyone ever thought up that aphorism about good fences making good neighbors is that fighting between homesteads is bound to break out; it is a perennial part of suburban life. The warring is constant. We fight over trees and walls and fences and garbage bins and sheds and garages and dogs and marauding teenagers. On one side of town, my children's stepmother, on the side of the angels, was uncharacteristically hysterical, weeping in impotent rage, phoning *The New York Times,* rallying the neighborhood around the scandal of her new neighbors' having taken a chain saw to many of the trees on their property; people drove from miles around to bear witness to the massacre of hundred-year-old oaks and pines and apples and maples and cedars, stumps oozing and draining in the amoral sunshine. (It ought to have occurred to me right then how lucky I was to live next to people who did not want to cut down the trees, but it did not.) Another friend was taking her neighbor to court over a renovation that resulted in massive and loud air-conditioning units being positioned just outside her living room windows, where there had once been a rose garden. Yet another had screamed at a neighbor about a very high, and very cheap, fence that effectively walled in her driveway. I began to pay careful attention to the grim newspaper accounts—from all over the world—of neighbors shooting and killing each other over hedges that were too high, or badly trimmed. Gardeners are a passionate (some would say hotheaded, or even addled) tribe, and like many tribal people, are obsessed with border disputes. People seemed constantly to be fighting, making up, breaking down again.

Of course, when the suburbanite isn't fighting, she might be graciously eyeing other people's gardens and houses, full of gratitude to those neighbors who bring beauty and whimsy to the neighborhood, who plant and nurture and protect what they are honor-bound to pass down to the next generation. Down the street from me, a neighbor has pruned and fed her tulip tree so that by June it is heavily laden with flowers; they scatter to the ground and I gather bouquets of the green and yellow blossoms when I walk home from the station at dusk. Did I say gracious? That perhaps does not include those of us who consult the Midnight Florist: the shadowy yet familiar self who leaves her bed and steals out under the cover of dark to tear off just a few of that neighbor's perfect lilacs (the clippers would make too much noise, and seem too deliberate, should the police arrive). Hers are so much fuller, richer, the sunshine is brighter at that corner, and, after all, she doesn't even seem to know what she has. Not that I would do that.

My time of warring seemed to have come, bountifully, for the tree that was driving me crazy belonged to the *other* uphill neighbors who lived behind me; the collapsed wall and the collapsing tree seemed linked in conspiracy. Suddenly, after fifteen years of ignoring the subject, it seemed as if I were being forced to renegotiate all my boundaries at once.

The maple was growing at the edge of our yards, and as it had grown, it had become more and more of a nuisance, branches splitting off and falling; seedlings planting themselves haphazardly and abundantly; the canopy becoming more and more dense. The tree was what I thought of as a "light hog." Its leaves were so thick as to be impenetrable, and as a result the straggling hedge of privet along the neighbor's backyard simply stopped growing once it hit the edge of the tree's canopy, whose reach was getting broader with each year. The plants on my side of the border were doing only a little better. Buyer, beware: those plants were chosen because they were tolerant of the shade, but I have found that tolerating is not the same thing, and does not produce the same results, as thriving. As a consequence, there was a large gap between our yards, as if someone had knocked a tooth out of what had been, at best, a reluctant smile. (This thing about tolerating and thriving holds for all living things; I made a mental note to discuss it with the True Love, who seemed to be having a problem discerning his own capacity for happiness from the comfort of a familiar apathy. As I saw things in *his* garden, he tolerated the deep shade of a secluded life when he could have thrived in my sunny engagement.)

To make matters worse, the neighbors, who were also new to town, had immediately set up the requisite swing set, built of cedar. But the swing set had a plastic slide. A large, duck-weed-green lick of plastic unfurled from the top and loudly swooped its way down, and naturally, its owners had positioned the slide not to face their house. Who would want to look at such a thing? It faced my house. It was so close to the edge of their lot—their lot being much higher than mine, as our houses are built on a hillside and I am at the bottom—that the thing looked as if it might simply lengthen a few more feet, some steamy night, and rascally slide the rest of the way into my garden.

Obviously, I had developed an exaggerated aversion to the plastic; I'm the first to admit it. But brightly colored plastic (and who decided that kids enjoy these colors anyway?) in the garden is one of my peeves, and my prejudice was reaffirmed when a friend came for lunch one day and remarked immediately on the proximity and ugliness of the sliding board. You know how, when you see a blemish, you cannot stop staring at it? Just as the ball will always find the weak fielder, as the True Love might put it, the fault becomes a magnet to the eye. That was what had happened to me. Whenever I went out to the Back Forty, my eye was drawn immediately to the green plastic slide and its attendant maple. I was obsessed.

The Boys did their best to talk me down out of that tree. They were passionate defenders of children's rights in the garden, which was, after all, their private playground. Flowers, shrubs, trees—all those got in the way of a good game of catch. The Boys pointed out, with that ruthless, intense rigor we so dislike in children, that we had once had a swing set ourselves, near the same corner of the yard (yes, but it was hidden among the hemlocks, my dears); that my idea that there be a swing set in only one person's yard, and that the children actually play with one another, was ridiculous; that no kid would ever want to have to get permission to swing in some-one else's yard, and grown-ups would never agree to share swing sets, what a stupid idea, Mom (why not? Why did every yard have to replicate the same debris, swing after swing marching down the backs of the houses?); that our swing set had been made of wood, too (yes, but so was the slide, a nicely understated slide, boys); that the wooden slide had lodged in one of their thighs a splinter the size of a dinner knife, and don't you remember how we had to go to the emergency room for stitches (we suffer for good taste, boys); that the sound of children was sweet, and are you getting old and cranky, Mom? (you children never screamed so loud, I wouldn't have permitted it—what happened to discipline?—and yes, damn it, boys, I am cranky); that the tree was beautiful and old and had been there as long as they had been in the house, as long as they could remember (exactly. Making a bigger and bigger mess. That was the problem).

Still, these new neighbors were a great improvement on the previous owners of the house, who were a churlish and nasty lot. The Boys and I used to refer to our up-the-hill neighbors as the Witch and the Bitch.

The Witch had owned the Victorian house catty-corner to mine; she was named the day she rained down curses angrily, from her window, at two little boys who had dared to turn their tricycles around in her driveway. She was to die a lonely death, in her bed, in the same old pile of a house in which she had been born, in which she had nursed her father through his last illness, in which her heart had been broken by her father's dashing and handsome doctor—one of those married men who think they are still single, and who, unluckily, turned out to be the one and only love of her life. After her heart broke, so went the lore among the old-timers, she never left the house, except to wander from time to time through the garden and onto the driveway, where she would stoop for hours pulling weeds up out of the pea gravel. (Actually, I saw her walk to the supermarket, for a couple of years, returning each day carrying a small plastic bag knotted at the handle—but who was I to contradict the village wags?) In the thirteen years that she was my neighbor, water never burbled through the ornate fountain that sat in the middle of the garden. No friend ever strolled the property with her, admiring the flower beds. No sun was ever taken on the curlicue of a bench in the corner of the yard. Though he lavished attention on the begonias with which he filled the bowls of the fountain every year, the swarthy ogre of a gardener—who spoke little English and often shook his fist angrily at the sky—barely kept up the rest of the garden.

The Witch could bear to see only one color, in her house and in her garden. She was fixated on all things red; her garden was crammed with crimson azaleas and snappy begonias and blazing geraniums and lollipops of cherry trees. At dusk I could see that her kitchen was painted pink, and the tattered silk curtains of the dining room were also rose-colored. Red, the color of hearts and valentines and love. Red, for the Chinese: luck. But red was also the color that meant STOP. Her love of red, with its vibrant flair, was in marked contrast with her wan face and sallow complexion, and what seemed to be a life whose pulse was all but extinguished.

We had only one conversation in thirteen years, as she rebuffed all greetings, and usually kept shut and locked a large black metal gate at the entrance to her front porch, in the middle of which hung an elaborate crystal chandelier. That dazzled me—a crystal chandelier hanging out of doors; that, and the red everywhere, gave me to understand that she had once had a life of glamour and flamboyance. Now, nothing could summon her to her door, not the rings of the mailman, or the meter man, or Halloween's small trick-or-treaters with their high-pitched entreaties. But one day, sensing a strange presence near me as I sat, reading, by the Back Bed, I looked up from my book, and there she was, in demure heels and a dress cinched at her tiny waist, a red silk scarf around her neatly coiffed head: feeble, pale, thin, her hand in its dainty three-quarter-length white kid glove holding the rough arm of her scowling gardener. I could see, from the well-formed bones of her face and her enormous dark eyes, rimmed in kohl, that she had once been beautiful.

"What is that?" she said, pointing to a bouffant of a camellia tree growing behind my house—the noble *Camellia japonica,* mind you, not the leggy *C. sasanqua,* so common that it is used as hedging in the South. I had no idea what hybrid was living in the garden, something semi-double, whose blossoms were full but not too ruffled. It was inexplicably thriving in our cold climate. It was spring, and flowers were bursting forth in all their symmetrical, round, elegant, and red, red, red glory. I always think of camellias as the most operatic of flowers, the Divas of Springtime: dramatic, intense, their passions unsustainable. I admired this one's upright posture, arms thrown heavenward, her glossy, deep green, leathery leaves—evergreen, improbably—her pale, fine, aristocratic bark, her bounty of blooms. Early each spring, along with the daffodils, the camellia would give generously of herself, until she languished into an exhausted swoon. Her flowers would plop, intact, to the ground at her feet; none of this petal-by-petal stuff for her. I had read somewhere that camellias represented longevity and faithfulness, and that a red flower symbolized intrinsic worth, and of course I believed all of this. Why not? Camellias were introduced here from Asia, where all flowers have such mystical qualities; it is part of their appeal. I was pleased that the camellia had drawn my neighbor's attention; I had a vanity about having coaxed it back to health after I found it, in an old bed in the backyard, in between two enormous mounds of hydrangeas, malnourished and entwined with the bittersweet vine that was the bane of my garden. Camellias don't usually grow so far north, and I assumed that the protection of my neighbor's carriage house had something to do with its happy life.

On pain of death, no one—and that meant greedy, inquisitive boys who took a cold, scientific interest in peeling apart those plump blossoms to see what was inside—no one was allowed to pick flowers off the camellia.

"This is a camellia," I said, and getting up from my chair, I went to the bush and snapped off a few blossoms for her. I gave the gardener the small bouquet, as my neighbor would not stoop to reach it (and you must understand that she stood on ground at least five feet higher than where I stood). The gardener smiled for the first time, and handed the bouquet to his lady. I looked up, waiting to see what she would say next, when suddenly she drew back, as if frightened, and threw the flowers down. Her face then contorted with anger, and she spat at me.

Perhaps a visit from a madwoman was inevitable, in that thicket of a garden. I only hoped she would not cast an evil spell.

The Bitch was the neighbor above and directly behind my house; she had owned the maple when the first of its many rotting limbs fell into my yard. Whereas the Witch's family had owned the Victorian since the 1890s, when it was built, the other neighboring house seemed to change hands frequently, no one staying more than a few years. Suffice it to say that one of its occupants was a woman who screamed constantly, at her children, her cats, her dog, her husband, and my children. One evening, from her yard, where she was weeding not ten feet away, my termagant neighbor watched me, very pregnant with my second child, lose my footing on the damp and slippery flagstone and fall flat on my back. Did she offer to help me get up, or inquire as to my injury? No. She laughed. And that was the last straw in our relations. (I describe all this lest you are harboring any remaining illusions that it is all roses in the suburban garden.)

The old neighbors had let everything they could not see from their windows fall into ruin. This meant that everything I could see right outside my windows was decrepit. Or worse. The carriage house, in its decline, at least had charm; the other neighbor's garage, also within the view of my kitchen window, had none. Its back wall had been forced open by the weight of a dead tree; holes in the foundation and an abandoned pile of rotting logs had become a dwelling for skunks; a clutch of weeds had sprouted up and become looming trees, *Ailanthus altissima,* known to highway embankments everywhere; they were called the Tree of Heaven, but they were the Tree of Hell to me. Every time a branch broke off, which was a daily occurrence, as these weed-trees were of a pathetically weak wood, a sulfurous smell rose up from the break. Every summer dozens of ailanthus sprouts tunneled into my garden, growing deliriously fast. All this was topped off with the bittersweet vine, *Celastrus orbiculatus,* introduced from Asia, an invasive twiner that girdles and kills whatever it climbs, and which thrives in exactly this kind of neglect. It had frothed its way up over the ailanthus, was clogging the privet, and from there scrambling into the uppermost branches of my dogwood tree. Bitter, as it is referred to, was fast becoming another one of my demons. It was brought to this country in the mid-1800s, and it quickly gained popularity for its use in crafts—like making baskets and wreaths. Its twisting growth is dramatic, and its bright saffron berries split open to reveal a cunning crimson-colored center. But the berries rapidly fall off the wreaths and sow themselves profusely. Bittersweet got out of control all over the country. It is impossible to kill. I give it grudging admiration; it is a survivor. Such tenacity had to be respected. No matter how much you pull up, no matter how much of the gnarled yellow root mass you claw up out of the earth—and this is a plant whose every inch fights the spade— the bitter grows back. It knows when to yield, sacrificing some of itself to certain death, keeping back just enough, hidden deep underground, to return with renewed vigor.

In short, the back quarters of my yard—really the neighbors' yards—were a mess, and hard to contain. As they were my borrowed view—not ten feet from my house, the part of the garden I saw first thing in the morning—I watched the mess metastasizing right outside my kitchen window. The weeds from the neighbors' yard were constantly threatening to overrun the Back Bed in front of the retaining wall. I was amazed at the speed with which things were deteriorating. Of course there was no talking to the old neighbors. I could only climb the wall and sneak into their yards whenever I could see they weren't around (I know, this is trespass) and hack away at the stuff tangled in my trees, trying to contain the damage. But weeding and skulking are incompatible postures.

I was beginning to feel that suburban neighbors were most useful when they moved. At least I had a quiet month or two, when there was a change in ownership, until closing, to do some cleaning up. One of my neighbors around the corner invited me to dig up an enormous tree peony and transplant it to my garden; she was leaving the country and could not count on her successors to appreciate what they had. Indeed, I have noticed, over and over again, that new suburbanites never wait a season or two to see what might be growing, and as they usually take possession of their houses before the school year begins, but after the blooming spring season, they generally think every shrub is a worthless bunch of sticks, and out come the garden crews with their chain saws. Perhaps there is something atavistic about the need for tabula rasa in suburbanites.

The ownership of both of my back neighbors' houses turned over at around the same time. Both sets of new owners were attentive when I visited to talk about the mess I was facing out my windows, though I could tell they were mildly annoyed at having to give a second's thought—much less a nickel—to property they would never see. So it was generous of them to offer to split with me the cost of cleaning up part of their yards. I was willing to do anything, by then, because really, the first thing you see in the morning is of utmost importance, and if it isn't the dear face of the True Love, it oughtn't to be someone else's weedy backside.

One afternoon—this was a few months after the retaining wall had toppled—another storm blew up. Because of the drought that summer, the yellowing of the sky and the wind lashing at the trees, bringing the first downpour in months, were a welcome relief. I shut all the windows, and sat in an armchair watching the drama. Suddenly the room was silvered with lightning, and there was a loud clap of thunder, followed by a terrible cracking noise. I looked anxiously at the front yard, afraid that one of the dozens of rangy sassafras had fallen over; they were all swaying wildly, but standing. The storm was brief, and when the rain let up I went out to the side garden to find the damage. An enormous limb had split off the neighbor's maple and crashed down onto their children's swing set, bashing in the dark green canvas tent that topped the slime-green sliding board. That, of course, was intact.

At that moment, something inside me snapped, too.

I had harbored my grudge against the umbrageous maple all winter; I was finally demented enough to pick up the phone and suggest to my startled neighbor that she would be wise to take the tree down. She protested that her husband had grown fond of it. It provided shade for the swing set. I protested that I had been told by the surveyor that it sat partly on my property line, and that therefore I might be legally responsible for any damage. But worse was the possibility that a branch might fall on a child. The sight of the limb in the swing set had loosened in me all the old rage at the tree. I began having nightmares about limbs chasing children through the streets, children becoming mired in a quicksand of melted plastic. Like I said: obsessed.

The next day, I drafted a letter to my neighbors, explaining why I thought they should take the tree down. I did not tell the Boys what I was doing, as they would have stopped me. And for once I was glad not to have the True Love around to talk to; he would have thought of hilarious ways to make things much worse. Pranks were one of his specialties. I was too far gone for anyone's help.

I told the neighbors that I wanted to clarify my thinking. My tone was tepid, my words insulting to the tree. Not very diplomatic. Norway maples are horrid, I wrote. They are trees, introduced into this country from Europe, that have become invasive. They are shallow-rooted, and compete with other plants in the landscape; on a large scale, they have been terrible for our Northeastern woods. They have forced out native species. On a garden scale, they are weak. They crack easily. They rot quickly. They do not share. The tree's roots were knocking down the stone wall between our yards. (Well, okay: my research also turned up the lovely fact that the density of their wood made it an excellent material for crafting the soundboards of musical instruments. It was rumored that the fiddlebacks of the celebrated violins produced in the seventeenth-century workshop of Antonio Stradivari were made of Norway maple. But I did not share this charming bit of information; who is making violins around here?)

I'm afraid that some of my bile had been enriched by doses of half-truths and misinformation about property rights and legal responsibilities from various Helpful Men, who had their own reasons for hating Norway maples, which have a tendency, in storms, to topple across the roads, pulling down power lines and crushing parked cars and blocking traffic. As everyone in suburbia knows, it rains only on Saturday or Sunday; this depredation generally happens on weekends in the middle of the night, and the Helpful Men are forced out of bed to chain saw the criminal trees.

"I've declared a vendetta against Norway maples," Leonard said grandly. "Do you want me to talk to them? Get rid of it, I say. Plant a nice red maple. Those Norways don't even turn a nice color in the fall. They just drop their leaves in a brown heap."

I duly reported this to my neighbor, as an argument that he should not be proud of having such a tree in his garden. I explained that I did not want to get into legalisms about the tree, but I wanted to find a solution to its menace that worked for both of us. (Of course, the only thing that worked for me at that moment was being rid of it.)

I added customary niceties about the cheering sound of children playing and laughing in the swings. (A bittersweet sound, in truth, for my children seemed to have outgrown their swing set so quickly; where did the time go? The sound of swing sets is the sound of lost childhoods—those of my sons, and mine, too. Every time the little girl shrieked with joy at the top of her ride, I remembered my sister and I as little girls on our swing set, pumping madly, getting as dangerously close as possible to looping right over the top, screaming with wild abandon. Why did we want to grow up so fast? Why must every six-year-old insist firmly that, no, she is not six, but six and three quarters, nearly seven.) The neighbors' daughter was a beautiful, moonfaced creature—she was, uncannily, her mother in miniature. She shrieked every time the swing went a bit too high, and then begged for more, as is the wont of

children everywhere. I wanted to be on good terms with these neighbors, who were pleasant enough.

I slipped the letter into their box. The reply, drafted on the New York City letterhead of a white-shoe legal firm, was immediate. Thus I learned that my neighbor was a lawyer. The tree was his, declared the neighbor; as he saw it, it was on his property almost entirely. He had tried to be a respectful neighbor, that was why he had agreed to incur some expense for cleaning behind his garage. As the letter went on, his language gathered steam. I felt as if I had disturbed a nest of wasps.

"I know that the statutes of New York provide for recovery of treble damages from anyone who cuts down, girdles, or otherwise despoils a tree on the property of another without the owner's leave . . . any cutting of the roots on your side with an intent to despoil the tree would be grounds for action under the same statutes and as a common law tort."

Niceties were returned.

By the end of the letter my brain was swimming. Legalisms had gone forth and multiplied. I surrendered. In truth, I was glad to have lost the battle. As soon as I had delivered my letter, I began to have sinking feelings about my suggestion to remove the tree. I had been extreme. I could have simply suggested judicious pruning. The tree was useful to me; it blocked out much of my neighbor's house, and his neighbor's house as well. It was a strange, tilted thing, whose branches had a weird sway to them. I believed it to be dangerous. But it was a tree, and it was held in regard by its keeper, and it had a right to live.

I had been reading about the Druids, and the other ancient cultures that worshipped trees as divinities in their own right. One particular passage in Sir James Frazer's *The Golden Bough* about the punishment set out in old German laws for

anyone who but dared to peel the bark of a standing tree, had made a vivid impression: "The culprit's navel was to be cut out and nailed to the part of the tree which he had peeled, and he was to be driven round and round the tree till all his guts were wound about its trunk." There was enough of the pagan in me to fear for my life in a trade for that of a tree.

And of course I could understand shade on a swing set. I needed shade, too, being intolerant of full sun. My new garden would just have to adapt to the maple.

But things had already been set in motion.

I replied by the next day's mail.

"Thanks for your speedy reply, and okay, okay! I don't think we need to discuss the poor maple any longer; you've heard the last of it from me. I am reassured to have you take full responsibility for it." Etc. and etc. I told him I understood about the children and shade, and that everything I would plant would thrive in shade as well. As did I. That of course, as he had decided to keep the tree—and was claiming ownership—I would not be girdling it or doing anything to damage it; that was not at all in my interest, since it could as easily topple into my garden as his. Not to worry, I was not a maniac (even though I sounded like one). That I was grateful to him for having agreed to clean the back of the garage; I understood it was not in his interest, and that I would gladly pay to keep the area weeded and pruned, so that they would not have the expense of maintaining a part of the yard they never saw.

I closed with more niceties, using up all the niceties I could think of. Brinksmanship has a way of curtailing goodwill.

The next day I received a letter from my neighbor describing a visit from a tree pathologist (requisite commendations of his authority and sound training attached), who had declared

the Norway maple sound and healthy, so my neighbor reported. Maples just dropped their limbs. That was how they were.

However, this same pathologist had noticed a hole in the noble, hundred-and-fifty-year-old pin oak that towered over my yard. Squirrels were nesting in it, and that meant the tree was decayed.

"I am afraid I must warn you about the tall pin oak that stands in your lot in a direct line with my children's play area . . . a strong storm wind or other powerful wind could knock the top of the tree off and turn it into a MISSILE aimed at our houses, other neighbors' houses and most frightening for me, my children's play area!"

The wasps, still buzzing angrily.

I replied that I would hire the same pathologist to assess the health of my oak (figuring it was safe to follow in a lawyer's footsteps), and that I would do everything to protect a valued, and valuable, tree. As to missiles flying into houses, I wrote, alas, nothing could be done. I suggested that if he were truly frightened of limbs falling on his children, he could move the swing set. (I refrained from adding that he might turn the slide around to face *his* living room window.)

His letter had continued to address my offer to weed the area behind the garage. It made him nervous, he said, because of a strange bit of law called adverse possession. "It seems that if you undertake weeding . . . for a long period of time back there, it could possibly cause a cloud on my title to that area . . ." He needed to "feel comfortable" by having me sign a copy of his letter which, he said, would represent "your acknowledgment that this is only a courtesy to you [strange courtesy, my being allowed to weed because they wouldn't], that you intend no adverse claim of title to the area. . . ." He asked that I return the signed copy in the self-addressed stamped envelope, which he furnished.

Stamped envelope, indeed. That, oddly, was the most insulting part. Still, adverse possession gave me a chuckle; it seemed like a most useful and inspired sort of phrase. Adverse? Yes. Possession? No. Adverse Disposal was on my mind. They could not have paid me to take that bit of property; being left with no recourse but to assume its care seemed like a good example of adverse possession. The phrase hovered at the edge of my thoughts for days. Could you take adverse possession of people, I wondered idly, and how vulnerable was the True Love? I gladly signed over my rights to the plundering of the back of his garage, in exchange for the right to keep it in order.

Niceties were added, and I mailed the document back in my own envelope, defiantly wasting his stamp.

And so, into my life entered Mr. D'Ambrosio—what a promising name for such a dreaded visitor—the tree pathologist. I called him several days later, and he agreed to come for a consultation. On the phone, he told me that he remembered the squirrels in the oak. He took a rather bleak view of the situation; when I remarked that the tree looked completely healthy, he said that trees can look great but be rotten inside, like people. Treatment could help, surgery could help; it depended. He had a scientific method for determining danger. He would need to take measurements.

"I just have to send my guys up into the tree, assess the damage. Maybe it's just a little hole, maybe the sort of thing we can block with a screen. But squirrels, you know, they chew right through screens. So we could put rocks in the hole, fill it up. That way, when the squirrels try to move back in, they think, hey, no way, this is too much trouble. They leave."

I was impressed with how far scientific treatments had advanced.

"But of course," Mr. D'Ambrosio went on, "if the tree is too decayed, it has to come down. No more structural integrity. Or, you prune it, so the wind goes through, not against. You know?"

I understood, and said I wasn't even going to consider the worst-case scenario. The tree was beloved; indeed, it is one of the things I am most pleased and proud to have inherited in this garden. Ah, beware vanity. The oak towered over the Back Forty. I had spent hours sitting under the tree on an uncomfortable little stone bench that was sinking and tilting— left there by the previous gardener—thinking things over. The oak seemed to have an oracular spirit; I communed with it, at the end of a day of work, as often as I could. The oak was a touchstone in my fantasy of how my garden would one day feel. The tree was so mythically tall that, by some mysterious visual alchemy, it actually made all the other trees around it look bigger than they really were—to my eye, at least. The oak animated everything else in the yard. And of course, being so large and having such a beneficent, paternal spirit, the oak made me feel especially small, like a child. From my bath, I gazed at one particular limb from season to season, following its gnarling growth, admiring its bare lines in winter; it ran, as if defying gravity, straight across the window at the foot of the tub. I had, until the visit from the plant pathologist, thought that I had taken good care of it. Apparently not.

"And your dogwoods, by the way," Mr. D'Ambrosio was going on. "A little thin on top. Trouble on top means trouble at the bottom. Could be a late case of anthracnose. Could be a root crown fungus. They're very susceptible to that. I don't know. I'll get in there. I'll give you a case-by-case assessment."

I was feeling very sorry I had ever called the doctor, the lawyer's footsteps notwithstanding. Perhaps it was not wise to rely on the lawyer's doctor; perhaps this pathologist had uncovered the disease between the neighbors, and was protecting himself from liability. I would have to get a second opinion, or a third. This was like a punishment from the gods; they were playing a grand joke. The tree I disdained was supposedly healthy; the tree I loved and admired was supposedly dying. I was feeling gloomy, surrounded by so much pathology; I didn't want to hear about it. I told him what people are always telling me. *Think positive! Hope for the best!*

"You gotta consider everything, young lady," Mr. D'Ambrosio said as our phone call wound down. "Hoping, that doesn't matter. I just check the trees and learn the facts. I'm warning you, though, if it's dead, I won't take it down. I don't take trees down. I'm a physician, not a mortician. But don't worry, I got guys who do that. I got guys for everything."

I hung up and went through the rest of the week with a heavy sense of dread; I felt as if I were waiting for lab results to return—well, I suppose I was, from Mr. D'Ambrosio's pathology brain. I just had to wait for him to find time on his schedule to see me. I was heartsick in anticipation. I did catch myself wondering, though—if the tree fell down on my house, did that give me an excuse to redesign the south side to include a conservatory?—only to stop myself; why tempt the fates?

How oddly things boomerang. Had I not riled up my neighbor, this pathologist would not have gotten him riled up about my oak. But then again, had he not noticed the squirrel's nest, I wouldn't have been able to do anything about it, and rot cannot be left to cloy its way through healthy tissue. And the tree would have died—if it wasn't already, in its majestic

youth, dying. Was this warning—if I was lucky and that was all it turned out to be—the unexpected gift in all the trouble I had caused?

My neighbor remarked one morning, weeks later, that he had learned an important lesson from our correspondence, a lesson about clear boundaries. I had learned it, too—or at least, I had learned that it was important to let those who needed to, think that there was such a thing as clear boundaries. The surveyor had located my property line in the middle of the remnants of an old stone wall at that end of the yard, so the maple seemed, in part, to spill onto my property. But the wall had become a useless borderline, as it was in a state of collapse. Where the roots of the tree had massed, the wall had been reduced to a pile of rocks. But by then I did not care for more agitation. I had learned to shut my mouth.

So much for trust between neighbors. I wanted to apologize for ever having suggested the removal of the tree, but due to legalisms, I did not, thinking that any admission that it was no longer a concern for me might cause me problems down the line. Legalisms have a way, I noticed, of stifling kindly impulses. I had brought this mess upon myself, wretch that I was.

I reviewed the whole sorry saga in the weeks that followed. I began yet another mighty and hopeless battle with the bittersweet—and where, exactly, is the sweet part of that scourge?—that was growing up out of the stone pile, once again strangling what was left of the neighbor's privet, hurling itself into my trees. The neighbor's gardeners had just that morning buzzed off the front of the privet, but naturally had avoided weeding it, or pruning the back side that faced me.

Anyone who has ever struggled with that nasty, strangling

vine will understand the rage I was in that morning, drenched with sweat, streaked with dirt, choking on leaf spores, my hair catching on twigs, my arms raked and bleeding from the sharp cut ends, my neck and shoulders twinging from repeated and useless attempts to pull the pest up by the roots. Even the tiniest tendril was deeply anchored.

My neighbor suddenly loomed over me, atop the wall, while his daughter played on her swings. He was wondering if I was sure, before I pulled it up, that there was nothing at all redeeming about bittersweet?

Bittersweet. How lucky I was, indeed, to have gotten permission to clean the back of the garage. A cosmic adjustment, perhaps, for having thought of cutting down a tree.

## THE VARMINTS

*"But I have no lethal weapon—*
*Thus does Fate our pleasure step on!*
*So they still are quick and well*
*Who should be, by Rights, in hell."*
—Dorothy Parker
"Frustration"

I had taken a late train home from work, and was walking up my driveway in the dark, when I saw a furry white stripe standing squarely in my path. Three more smaller striped balls of fur trailed behind, not watching where they were going—watching me—and bumped one after another into their mother. Luckily, because my driveway is in such disrepair, I was moving slowly, picking my way through stony trenches. Otherwise I would have stumbled over my visitors, with dire consequences—for me. *My* visitors? The skunks were looking at me as though I were the intruder. I stopped in my tracks; they did not budge. We were in a face-off. It lasted all of five seconds. I slowly began to retreat, not an easy feat, feeling my way backward across the mossy ruts. I did not turn my back on the skunks until I got to the bottom of the driveway, and I crossed the street to watch them from a safe distance. They stood their ground a little longer, then, one by one, waddled home. Home, I noticed, happened to be under my kitchen stoop.

My garden is plagued by skunks. And raccoons, opossums, rabbits, squirrels, gophers, moles, and mice. I expect to see deer get off at the train station any day now. Worse yet, I had the suburban version of all these animals—fatter, meaner, smellier, messier, lazier, and more aggressive than their country counterparts. Right at home in our yards, in our garages, in our driveways, in our garbage cans. Theirs is not a peaceable kingdom. They fight with each other, and with every poor cat or dog or toddler that gets in their way. They fight over the territory, they fight over the grubs, they fight over the birds' eggs, they fight over the chicken bones and pizza rinds. They even fight over scraps of tissue and tinfoil.

It is not a nice way to begin the day, in your nightgown in the driveway, righting and refilling a stinking garbage can that has been knocked to the ground, its contents shredded into impossibly small bits, strewn across the yard, blowing and rolling into the street. There is no such thing as a locking garbage-can top. Raccoons are much smarter than children, who are flummoxed by garbage cans, unable to figure out how to remove the top when they are asked to take out the trash.

Raccoons know exactly what to do, no matter what top you give them. Raccoons cannot wait to take out the trash.

The raccoons seem to own the garbage cans, but the possums have taken over the garage, which is where the garbage cans are stored. (I cannot figure out how they get in, but a deeply clawed bit of wood near the door might be a clue.) This has led to gang warfare, which means hair-raising shrieks and growls erupting in the middle of the night, loud enough to raise the dead, let alone the insomniacs.

The raccoons come out into the garden earlier and earlier, no longer waiting for dark, and this has emboldened everyone else to join in and make an appearance at the cocktail hour. My sister, sipping a glass of wine with me in the garden one evening, jumped and screamed and pointed over my shoulder, and I turned slowly to see a big, handsome, masked devil of a raccoon standing, one paw on his hip, I swear, as if to say, *Come on, girls, drink up. Closin' time.*

The possums are slothful. It is not enough for them to camp out in the garage, they must make a mess of everything in there as well. They have mauled the bags of peat moss, clawed the car, and I am sure they were the ones who punctured the bicycle tires. So what, they can hang by their prehensile tails? What is this, the circus?

The squirrels scrabble and die in the walls of the house. They drop down the chimney. They ravage the roots of potted plants. I have never seen such feats of derring-do as those performed by squirrels chasing one another, such graceful acrobatics, such frisky scampering—all to move a nut from one hole to another. Yes, this is the circus.

The mice chew through bags of rice and cereal in the pantry. I could not understand how they got into the house, until one day, while I was doing the dishes, I saw a mouse walk boldly through the back door, which I had left ajar to get fresh air, and climb the stairs into the kitchen. The mice winter in the leather palms of my gardening gloves, and for refreshment nibble on the fingertips.

The bunnies lollop adorably.

And the crows. Their raucous, predawn gossip just outside my window every morning left me half-crazed. I would get out of bed, go out on the balcony, reach into the bucket of rocks I kept by the door for just such purposes, and hurl them into the trees. It was useless. They would fly in just as the sun was rising, about a dozen of them, and take their places in the sassafras, in the most orderly fashion, and scream and caw for twenty minutes. You could set a clock by their arrival and departure. I had once liked crows, when I was a child. My father used to call them into the yard, throwing his head back, opening his throat and cawing and crackling loudly and wildly, unstoppable, in the most realistic fashion, until dozens of the black creatures would be flapping frantically about him. He seemed to become a crow before our very eyes. (My father also taught me how to sing through my thumbs exactly like a dove; it only takes one glass of wine to get me to demonstrate this remarkable talent.)

But these predawn visits from the crows were maddening.

Then suddenly they were gone; they never returned. I read in the papers a few days later about the discovery of a cornfield upstate littered with dead crows, hundreds of them, killed by the West Nile virus. I'm sure my crows were among them, and though I don't miss their racket, I would trade it anytime for the dawning of such a virulent disease on our shores.

The skunks will eat garbage, if the raccoons are serving that night, or grubs, and in my garden they have the luxury of picking and choosing. My lawn, what is left of it, is riddled with the bullet holes the skunks create with the pointed tips of their fossicking noses. They waddle around, heads low, sniffing out the night's delicacies. Have you ever seen a grub move? I never have; they don't, to our eyes. And I have never heard a grub say a word, but the skunks, with their sharp ears, hear everything that is going on under the ground, every curl and cry, and they drill their way rudely into the middle of the conversation, swallowing up every last grub faster than they can say *Help!* Those skunks could probably hear the grass grow. If they would let it grow. It has become my morning ritual, coffee in hand, to patrol the shredded lawn to see what fresh holes have been drilled overnight. I, who never before cared about her lawn, am now furious at the skunks' incessant, havocking trespass. (I have one friend who actually claims to like the smell of skunks—well, only when it is quite faint. It reminds him of the scent of marigolds. Who likes the scent of marigolds? I haven't yet met the sweetly lemony ones. You can put marigolds on my Prejudice List.)

Skunks, unlike raccoons, seem incredibly stupid, but what do I know? I just assume they don't need any smarts. They don't have to think about anything. All they have to do is react. One summer three of them wandered to the edge of a basement window well and fell in, landing on top of one another in a stack. Of course they sprayed in fright, and then couldn't climb out. All three died there. The smell got into the basement, and lingered for a year. There is no such thing as a deodorizer that kills skunk odors, no matter what the nice people at the hardware store tell you. Skunks, unlike the perfumers for whose evanescent goods we pay a small fortune, have perfected the staying power of a scent. The skunks in the window well were there for weeks before I found them. I had been away from home and it took me a while to trace the source of the vomitous stench around my house—fear and death mixed. When I found them in the well, I went down to the basement where I could see them from the other side, sandwiched between the concrete and the window glass, and I really should not have stared at them for so long; I became mesmerized by that catacomb, and the vision will haunt me forever.

It is not a nice way to end the day, eyes stinging, nose prickling and running, precious dreams of the True Love promptly evaporating, as droplets of a skunk's spray waft up two floors on a cool night breeze and in through the window, drizzling down on you, peacefully asleep, in your bed. Well, you *were* asleep. There is no rest after that. After that it is time to stand on the balcony hurling rocks at the gorgeous enemy, glowing in the moonlight. Another useless activity, by the way. I am ready to call in the nematodes, but I know that my skunks will simply develop a taste for the very creatures that kill the grub. I am hopeless. The skunk, as far as I am concerned, is a case study of the neurotically evolved animal, and it ought to be widely rounded up for clinical observation. It is the flawless exemplar of the passive-aggressive character, lethally combined with every single classic attribute of a borderline personality disorder. It provokes aggravation, drives everyone around it nuts, and remains happily oblivious, perfectly content to be the small, furry, placid, narcissistic center of others' misery.

Whose garden is this, anyway?

I suppose you could say it had once belonged to the animals, and that we had intruded on their natural habitat. True enough. And with more and more land being developed into suburbs, there was less and less room for the animals to live.

Their natural predators, red foxes, wolves, coyotes, had been driven farther into the wilds, or extinguished altogether, and there was nothing left, save the hawks, to control the exploding population of the creatures. Unless you count cars.

And in one of those stunning turnabouts that only Mother Nature can whip up, the animals were back, intruding on our habitat, with a vengeance. No suburban garden was safe from the depredation of the animals. They had adapted to our foods, our houses, and our gardens. They were more than happy to tunnel under foundations, nestle among trees, eat leftovers. They were even beginning to alter their hours—hunting no longer took all night, so why not start early and get in a little more shut-eye?

We were in close quarters, in suburbia, with the animals. Too close.

The wildlife in the garden seemed to bring out the predatory streak of the suburbanites. Talk at cocktail parties or cookouts frequently turned to the animal problem, and it revealed a side of my neighbors that haunted me—a bit. It was at a block party that I learned that one couple frequently trapped skunks in a contraption they bought from a hardware store, put them in a plastic bag, and attached the bag to the exhaust pipe of their car. Another confessed—bragged?—that he had arrived at a method of killing animals after realizing that trying to suffocate skunks in garbage bags seemed ineffective; they simply went into hibernation and woke a few weeks later when the bag was opened. Now he drowned them in garbage cans full of water. Another borrowed a paint gun from his brother—not too far removed from my Annie Oakley fantasies with a BB gun.

One afternoon, as I was weeding, a possum waddled past in a hurry; right behind him were three little boys—no more than seven years old—wielding large baseball bats. I was horrified at their bloodlust, but took some comfort in the way the boys hung back, looking more fearful than their prey that they would succeed.

The animal problem in suburbia was not bringing out the best in anyone.

One day Leonard came over, with a couple more Helpful Men who were installing a watering system. They were old friends; they talked about their wives, their children, sports leagues, and school buddies. They had started laying out the system weeks earlier, but a hose had already broken and water was puddling in the driveway. Fred quickly located the source of the gusher, and pulled the severed hose out of the ground.

"Will you look at that?" said Leonard. "Chewed right through. You can see the tooth marks."

We had been in a long drought, and while I was watering abstemiously, the animals were guzzling. I told the men of my plague of trouble.

"I ought to bring over a pop gun, give you a few lessons. You need to get rid of some of these critters. That's the only way to do it," Leonard said.

"Isn't that illegal, Leonard? Firing a gun in a garden in Westchester?"

"Aw, well, no one needs to know—"

He was interrupted by Fred.

"Yeah, Leonard, you are such a he-man. He'll kill your skunks, all right. I won't tell the story of taking my son fishing in the boat with you. Will I?"

Leonard shrugged his shoulders. Fred told the story.

"We're out in the boat, we're catching fish, small ones, sunnies? porgies? My son, he's nine, he wants to know what do you do with them after you catch them. Leonard takes a fish, it is thrashing like crazy in his hands. Leonard bites off the head, spits it out. The thing is still moving. Blood is running down Leonard's chin, down his shirt. Fish blood. I nearly got sick. I nearly threw up. I wasn't ready for that."

The talk of hunting skunks had stirred up excitement. Fred was on a roll. Fred is a handsome, trim, dark-haired, well-muscled man. His brother has one of the sweetest faces I have ever seen. He looks like a pudgy, gray-haired, pony-tailed child. He had been working quietly at the back of their van, cutting a new section of pipe. Fred's brother has an enormous red heart tattooed on his arm, with an arrow piercing the side, and a scroll underneath, emblazoned with the name POPS. Their father had died a year earlier, and the grief-stricken sons still couldn't bear to return to his house. Fred turned to his brother.

"Yeah, what a he-man," Fred said. "Better than when you took your nephew hunting."

Fred's brother looked up from his tubing. "I told him I'd take him anywhere, anywhere but there, to Pops's house. But no, he has to go to that house. Deer everywhere, but the kid only wants to go to Pops's house."

"Up at three in the ayem to get to Dutchess County to shoot deer," Fred went on. "Deer, you can hunt 'em by sitting on the shoulder of any road. You don't even need to hunt 'em. You pick 'em up. Their carcasses litter the highway."

Fred's brother was wincing, but he gamely picked up the story. "We pull in at the house, the kid's all excited, we catch a huge herd in the headlights, the animals scatter and run across the fields. So we sit and wait."

"They sit and wait," said Fred. "You sit. In the van."

"Yeah, why not? It's cold outside. It's dark. The deer are gonna be everywhere. They already *were* everywhere."

"In the van. The two of you. With the radio blasting, and the heat going, the headlights shining—"

"—so we could see them—"

"—drinking Coke, and you're waiting for the deer to appear?"

"Yeah. They never came back. We never saw another one."

It was past time to call the exterminators. And that was when I learned that they no longer exterminate. They control. They are professionals who practice pest control, which, when I finally found the listings in the phone book, sounded dubious, more like traffic controllers who suggest alternate flight plans. Pest control involves setting up traps so obvious that even the stupid skunks would not climb in. Why would they, when they could walk around to the back side and nibble the marshmallows through the wires of the cage?

Yes, marshmallows. It turned out that the suggested bait for luring skunks away from grubs was marshmallows, and cat food. The pro finally arrived, from New Jersey, in a large van that looked promisingly like the sort of thing a homicidal lunatic would live in, crammed with pillows, wire hangers, sharp tools and rubber gloves and traps and plastic sheets and filthy, torn overalls and half-eaten peanut butter and jelly sandwiches and bags of potato chips (for the drivers). He set up three traps, two the size of a shoe box and, because I insisted that no suburban skunk would fit into those little things, one larger one. He pushed a can of cat food to the back of the small traps, and baited the large trap with marshmallows, which did look delicious, bright white squares gleaming brilliantly in the twilight. I crossed the lawn to warn the neighbors not to let their children be tempted.

Did I say that I had to pay $180 cash *up front* for this service?

I went to bed that night feeling hopeful. I woke at dawn the next morning, like a child frantic to see what Santa had left behind. The traps were empty—of animals and of bait. I called Pest Control Headquarters to complain. An elderly woman with a tough tone in her thin voice answered.

"Animal must have reached in and got the bait," she said.

"But they aren't supposed to reach in. They are supposed to get trapped inside. I am not running a restaurant here. I am not trying to feed everybody. I am trying to get rid of them." I was becoming hysterical.

"Listen, lady. You said you got skunks. Skunks don't reach in. Raccoons reach in. They're big. Probably a raccoon reached in. They stretch their arms to the back of the trap and get the food. You told us skunks. So, you got raccoons? Or you got skunks?"

"I have *everything*," I said. "And I want traps that catch everything. I don't want useless little traps that feed everything. By the way, what do you do with the animals if you ever catch them?"

"We catch them, miss. We have a ninety-five percent success rate. We release them into the wild. You said skunks. Not raccoons."

Of course I was powerless, having already paid for this service. She agreed to send someone out to refill the cages.

The next night, I went to bed feeling like a Canadian settler, wondering anxiously if I would lure anything into my traps. I pondered the release factor, wondering if "the wilds" could mean a short waddle from my house, into the wooded highway embankment running along the banks of what was left of the clouded, clogged, and sluggish Hutchinson River. That, or the back of my neighbor's garage.

The next morning, I made the rounds; the small trap, once

again, had been emptied of cat food. What a disgrace. But, there in the large trap, filling it entirely, was a raccoon, who had finished her satisfying main course from the small trap and wandered over to the large one to see about that marshmallow dessert. The raccoon was making whirring, trilling noises, sounding rather like a dove, but at least two octaves lower. It was so plaintive, I wanted to release it but didn't dare. One of the Boys came into the garden to look at the trap.

"How would you like it, Mom, if I were caught and moved to another part of the country, and you didn't know where I had gone? Kidnapped. You wouldn't like it one bit. Would you?"

How could I tell him that the animals didn't feel that way about families? What did I know? It certainly sounded like this raccoon was upset. She interrupted her keening only to put her face into the tin of food and lick every last, moist crumb from the corners.

Several birds were in the trees overhead screeching at the raccoon. I don't think it was in sympathy for her plight, as I am sure enough of their hatchlings had disappeared down that fat thing's throat. I asked Theo how he felt about baby birds. The raccoon was now resting on her back, her paws holding the ceiling of the cage. She looked comfy.

I called Headquarters.

"So. Raccoons. I told you, miss."

"I need bigger traps. If the raccoons are eating the skunks' dinner before the skunks get to it, I will never catch the skunks. I need skunk traps that the raccoons cannot raid."

"You caught the raccoon. You have skunk traps."

It was Kafkaesque. I gave up. Several more nights went by, with the bait emptying from the traps. I stopped calling the professionals. I sent my son to the supermarket for more marshmallows and cat food, and reset the traps myself. We caught another raccoon. We caught two possums. True to form, they rolled over and played dead as soon as I came near the trap. The pros took them away.

The skunks remain at large.

# EIGHT

# DEATH OF THE HEMLOCKS

*"The way a crow*
*Shook down on me*
*The dust of snow*
*From a hemlock tree*

*"Has given my heart*
*A change of mood*
*And saved some part*
*Of a day I had rued."*
——Robert Frost
"Dust of Snow"

During the Winter of Last Daydreams, all but one of the
remaining hemlocks died. There had been at least

thirty of them when I had purchased the house. They had been planted, all squeezed together, in a ragged line (very suburban) at the side of the garden, to provide a screen from the neighbors' house. They didn't seem that old, maybe forty years, but perhaps, even in those days, something was broken down and needed to be blocked from view in that neighbors' driveway.

A few more hemlocks had been planted in front of an old brick barbecue grill, the sort of thing that was built in thousands of suburban gardens in the fifties, giving rise to countless jokes and cartoons of men in aprons and oven mitts poking meat over a fire, Man the Griller being a natural evolutionary step from Man the Hunter. The barbecue was in a sorry state, and by the time I moved into the house its various ovens and cubbies, stacked one on top of another, seemed to be serving as an apartment terrarium for all sorts of snakes and rodents. I considered whether or not to keep the barbecue, simply to rebuild it at some point in the future, as it then would be grandfathered from any village code prohibiting such a dangerous contraption. But it was located so far from the house that I would be making dinner with the neighboring musician and his mother, and the hemlocks that had been dotted around to screen it from view, probably no more than two feet high when they were planted in the fifties, were now trees twenty or thirty feet high, and their leaves looked suspiciously dessicated. I couldn't imagine lighting a fire underneath them. The barbecue was carted away. I have never missed it.

The hemlocks were ungainly. They had been topped earlier in their lives, which means their tops had been lopped off, a common practice among some of the so-called professionals who prune trees, in the belief that cutting off growth at the top will encourage a fuller shape below. It usually doesn't work that way—with hemlocks, and with most trees. It simply maims them. Instead of filling out, the hemlocks had sent two trunks up from just below the cut of the original, growing in a horseshoe configuration at the top of the tree. It looked weird.

Still, in the eighties, when we first moved in, the hemlocks had made a pleasant little grove, and, though thinning, provided shade and some buffer. I had looked them up in my plant encyclopedia: *Tsuga canadensis.* The branches had a discreetly lilting swag to them, the flat sprays of their foliage were graceful, their cones tiny; the leaves, only half an inch long, were soft, with two thin, elegant white pinstripes running the length of the underside; the dead needles laid a lovely ochre carpet at their feet. The birds loved the hemlocks, and frequently nested in the crooks of their limbs. The bark was a beautiful and unusual color, a mauve gray outside that, when scraped, showed a ruddy cinnamon brown that turned coppery in the late-afternoon light.

There was an abrupt switch in the plantings from the front garden to the side yard, from a clump of sassafras to a clump of hemlock, that bothered me when we first moved in, and then, as with all things in the side yard, I learned to ignore it. There was simply too much to do. As I said, I was treating this part of the yard as the Back Forty, which means I had given myself permission to let it go.

The shade was dappled under the hemlocks, but nothing was growing beneath them, and I didn't plant anything either. I enjoyed the shade as a place to sit and read. My father built a triangular tree house (for himself as much as for the children), bracing it in the trunks of three of the hemlocks, and the boys and I climbed into it and spied unseen on the musician and his mother, and the people passing in the street below. Nothing beats the pleasure of a tree house, especially when a honeysuckle vine clambers in, and you can pinch off the end of a blossom and suck out the delicious nectar. As the years went by, the hemlocks looked sadder and scrawnier, but it took a while for me to understand that this wasn't because I was sad and projecting my mood onto everything I saw. It was because the trees were dying.

In front of the hemlocks, closer to the house, stood three handsome dogwood trees. Native to North America, they are called *Cornus florida,* which means "flowering," and has nothing to do with the state. The trees were each about thirty feet tall. I would guess they were of the same vintage as the hemlocks. Now, most of the dogwoods that are being sold and planted are Asiatic in origin, arriving here from China, Korea, and Japan. Called *Cornus kousa,* they are of an altogether different nature from the American variety. The Oriental dogwood grows in an upright, vase-shaped fashion that rounds out as it ages, and its plentiful flowers, usually white (and not really flowers, but that's a technicality that doesn't matter to those admiring their beauty), arrive only after the leaves have come in, a month later than the American dogwoods, usually in early summer. Their show, and it can be extravagant, is of a creamy white set against a rich, ribbed green leaf. Korean dogwoods thrive in sun, and do not even pretend to tolerate shade.

The American dogwood lives in conditions opposite of those of its cousin. It thrives in shade but tolerates sun. Its flowers—actually bracts, which are modified leaves that turn color—present themselves early in spring, long before the green leaves think of unfurling. The blooming of the dogwood is a seasonal theatric. The dogwood's growth pattern is layered, branches spread in an umbrella-like fashion—think of umbrellas torn into quarters, and staggered one on top of the other up a central trunk. It is a candelabra of a tree. The branches of some trees arch and droop magnificently to the ground. You can stay dry under a healthy dogwood's canopy in an all-out rainstorm, and I have. There is nothing more breathtaking than the white blooms of a dogwood glowing in the moonlight; they look like stars fallen from the heavens, hovering just over our heads.

Dogwoods and hemlocks are among the trees that define the feel of the forests of the Northeastern states. Hemlocks were once much-valued trees. In colonial logging days, hemlock bark was a source of tannin for the leather industry. Its wood is soft and light, so that was used as pulp for paper. Native Americans used the cambium layer of the tree as food, mixed into breads and soups, and drank an infusion of hemlock needles, full of vitamin C. They made poultices to treat rheumatism and arthritis. I learned the hard way, with a few burns in the carpet, that hemlock is useless for firewood; it pops violently and spits showers of embers. (And no, Socrates did not die of this kind of hemlock poisoning; the one that took his life was an herb.)

Why did we ever lose our appreciation for all that a tree can give us? We took the dogwoods into our gardens for their elegant beauty and their promise of spring—how wonderful, a beauty that does not wait for the party to start, and arrives in her rustling *peau-de-soie* satin, ahead of everyone else, to whisper her warm promises. The dogwood is what nurserymen refer to as "an important ornamental." Suburban trees are not the same as country trees; because they are grown in proximity to houses and flower beds, they are much more demanding visually—they are not seen off in the distance, outside the wall of the cutting garden. Their placement is tricky; all sorts of things, like the eventual spread of the canopy and the sensitivity of the root system, have to be taken into consideration when placing trees in a suburban garden. A suburban tree is more coddled than its country cousins; I was struck, during a visit to the True Love's house in the country, that while I was fretting over the fate of one oak, one maple, and three dogwoods, his land was covered with oaks and maples and birches, all in various stages of growth or decay, some of them toppling over, limbs broken and sagging, some healthy and young and upright. There were so many trees that it was impossible to get tangled up in the fate of any one of them, impossible to personalize, impossible to lavish attention on any one character; there was room, in the countryside, for the natural order of things, room to accept death and disease and desuetude. I had no room for that in my suburban patch—as soon as death arrives, it is carted away. But whether I liked it or not, could tolerate it or not, the natural order of things was taking over.

We took hemlocks into our gardens for their light-handed evergreen usefulness. Both dogwoods and hemlocks quickly became staples of suburban gardens all the way down the East Coast to Florida, and as far north as Michigan and Ontario. And they thrived. When you piled into the family car and took a drive in spring through the towns of Georgia or New York or New Jersey or Connecticut or Pennsylvania, to gawk at the showy spring colors of the azaleas (and the tulips and daffodils and hyacinths and viburnum and forsythia and all the rest), whether the suburbs were a hundred years old or twenty years old, you would invariably see, in most gardens, a prized dogwood or two, debauched in pink or elegant in white. If you took your drive ten years ago.

All through our suburban plots, and in the forests of the Catskills and the Adirondacks, the hemlocks and the dogwoods, the trees that give these places their distinguishing features, are disappearing. For the last thirty years, slowly at first, then with accelerating force, death has overtaken these two of our favorite trees. Many nurseries stopped selling the American natives, because there is every possibility they will not last a year. No one knows exactly why they have become so vulnerable. We know what is killing them. Dogwoods are succumbing to an extraordinarily virulent epidemic, a ravaging dogwood anthracnose, caused by a fungus (*Discula destructiva*—how's that for an apt name, right up there with Cruella De Vil). The fungus was identified in the seventies and out of control by the nineties. One theory adds a strange political irony to the disease, for the dogwood anthracnose arrived on our shores in the early seventies when relations opened up with China, and we began to import Oriental dogwoods, which may have hosted the fungus without being vulnerable to it.

Hemlocks are being haunted by an evil succubus, the woolly adelgid. Presumably these are predators that, up until now, the trees were able to resist; the woolly adelgid was introduced into the States from Asia in the twenties but only began to wreak havoc recently. Scientists suspect that the trees' susceptibility has been brought on by everything from global warming to acid rain to, simply enough, the natural order of things. All too formidable for a forester in the Catskills, much less a suburban gardener, to combat. It's likely thousands more trees will die over the next five years.

This village was once full of hemlocks and dogwoods. I have watched, in garden after garden over the last decade, as one by one the grand old dames have blackened, died, and

been cut down. Replaced, frequently, by the Oriental dogwood, which is much less susceptible to anthracnose. Or, in
the case of the dying hemlocks, by the hearty, good-natured,
dime-a-dozen arborvitae, today's most common screening
tree.

In my own garden, the arborist was arriving every spring to
take down two or three more hemlocks that had not survived
the winter. The dogwoods, with me feeding and watering and
pruning, seemed to be hanging on. I watched the tips of their
uppermost branches for the telltale signs of trouble. But nothing helped the hemlocks. They became wrapped in woolly
white coats as the adelgid took them over. This insect clamps
onto the needles and branchlets and feeds on the tissue that
conducts food. I heard about washing the trees in an oily
solution that is meant to repel or smother the evil bugs, but at
least in my garden, that was a useless exercise. Nothing could
stop their dying but the eventual development of their own
resistance to the invader. Meanwhile, we were reading in the
papers about the devastation of entire forests in the Catskills.
A hike in the woods no longer held the same mysteriously
dappled, softly lit magic. I had never truly appreciated the
beauty of the hemlocks, never really singled them out to
admire, until they were dying.

Within ten years, most of the hemlocks in my yard were
gone. This was a vivid illustration of why it is not good to plant
too much of one plant in a small garden. It is vulnerable to
being entirely wiped out. By the end of the Winter of Last
Daydreams, only one hemlock was left standing. It was a
beauty. It was the only one that had never been topped—I
have no idea why it had been spared the fate of its mates—so
its trunks, and it had three of them, two smaller ones snuggled
at the side of the main one, grew straight and tall. The tree had

clearly been through a struggle, and its foliage was thin. I thought I might prune away the smaller trunks, to let the tree strengthen at the main one, but I didn't dare give it any more trauma from which to recover. Still, it was alive. And little by little, the hemlock seemed to grow stronger. Seeing that there was hope for its unlikely survival, I began to cheer the tree on. It was shaking off its enemy, becoming resistant before my very eyes, defying the fate of all the hemlocks with which it had grown up—as of this writing.

We shall see. But the resilience of the surviving hemlock— and the memory of walking among the many hemlocks— clarified my idea, that winter, of how I wanted my new garden to feel. If I had located the genius of my suburban garden, it was, in typical fashion, a genius being wiped out—one that caught my fancy as it was leaving, like the guest at a party you had meant to talk to, who departed early. But enough ghosts hung back to fire my imagination, and I needed plenty of that to impose character on this yard. I wanted more woods. I wanted my trees back.

Any garden is a sheer act of will, of course. It's just that in the suburban garden, there is usually very little at hand to enhance your first efforts. But that's also the beauty of suburban gardens. You are freed from natural constraints, providing there is enough rain. You can grow a blousy English garden right next door to a formal rose garden; you can give the neighbors something topiaried to talk about; you can stick to native, drought-hardy plantings; you can walk down the street past a modernist arrangement of only three kinds of plant, massed and repeated at regular intervals.

In homage to the remaining hemlock, and, as well, the stand of sassafras trees in the front—which, as the True Love once said dryly, only *I* could call a forest, so I suppose I won't—I decided to plant a walk in the woods. Like I said, imagination required.

The dogwoods will have to hang on. And I don't know what I will do if the sole surviving hemlock dies.

NINE

# IN THE HOLE

*"He made a pit, and digged it,*
*and is fallen into the ditch which he made."*
—Psalms 7:15

I had once completely given up on the Back Forty. It just seemed too difficult an undertaking to change the conditions under which I was supposed to revive that part of the garden. I was intimidated by what I had to work with—and that included lots of rock. I tried to plant some ground cover under the hemlocks, and couldn't get my shovel in deep enough to make a decent hole. I figured I would have to live with what was there: a mess. Probably not the best approach; as an architect once said to me, looking at a stone wall that I had assumed would be the demarcation for an addition to a house, "Just because the wall is there doesn't mean it has to be there." That remark was profound and should have been liberating, but I could not live up to it. When I see a wall, I do not always knock it down or clamber over it. I stop.

And so, during the years after my divorce, as I sat around in the Back Forty, contemplating the expansive, shelflike slabs of rock that revealed a bit more of themselves with every rainstorm, I was preparing to surrender to a barren land-scape. I felt, myself, very much like C. S. Lewis's block of stone, registering only the intense pain of my life being chiseled out by a relentless Creator. This was the path to happiness? The hemlocks were dying; who could fight death? How their roots had ever navigated the stony soil was beyond me, but I was sure it could never happen again.

My pessimism about the growing conditions in my garden had been confirmed years earlier, when I had first moved into the house. I had called a professional landscape designer from a fancy northern-Westchester nursery to see if he could give me some ideas for shrubbery to plant under the thinning hemlocks. The designer barely deigned to put me in his cal-endar when he heard that my garden occupied less than half an acre—and the part that I wanted him to help me with was only a third of that. Have you noticed how, these days, you no longer interview the professionals to see if you want their help? They interview you, to see if you are worth helping. I have had designers request photographs of my yard, its dimensions, the outer limits of my budget, and even my color preferences—as if, God forbid, I might want to implicate them in a red, yellow, and orange scheme—before they would agree to meet me. (Sure, I could pull the editor-of-a-magazine-that-covers-your-world card in introducing myself, but something about the need to do so is perversely humiliating, and I refuse.)

The designer, who, after all, was employed by a nursery whose business it was to sell plants, as I reminded him, hinting vaguely about unlimited budget and taste, finally agreed to meet me in my yard one afternoon. I left work early, got home in plenty of time, and started waiting. Two hours later, I was about to give up, when a car limped up to the sidewalk. The designer was in a fury. He had gotten lost in this unknown territory, a tire was going flat, he thought his car would give out, what a waste of time.

Not the best way to begin the consultation. His rage did not abate the rest of the half hour; he simply added a dollop of disdain. He tromped through the front yard to the side of the house where the hemlocks were languishing and pronounced them worthless. They were all going to go, he told me. Which I knew, and didn't need to hear with such violent smugness. I asked him about replanting. He took a metal probe out of the trunk of his car and began to poke around all over the side of the yard. "Impossible," he said after a few minutes. "You will never be able to plant another tree here. Not without using dynamite. There is too much rock. I don't use dynamite. Good-bye."

And that was that.

I could have used some dynamite right then. I felt a cascading loss of self-confidence. But the solution was obvious. Having had my garden rejected by one high-end professional, I vowed never to call another. I prefer to deal with the lesser mortals, to whom I am just one of those pain-in-the-neck female customers in town. I resigned myself to doing nothing to replace the dying trees. Perversely dying from the ground up. My view of the neighbors' old tires, dead battery, and rotting VW bus opened up grandly.

Years passed. Just as I was entering the Winter of Last

Daydreams, I happened to tell this story to a friend, an artist who was passionate about landscaping. Artists, I have found, are remarkably capable of ignoring the borders of impossibility. Back to those walls that didn't have to be there.

"Nonsense," said the Artist, when he heard of the verdict delivered on my plot of land. "Anything can be planted. If you can't dig, you can build up. And I'll bet you can dig."

As had others before him, he began to poke and prod the ground. But he pronounced himself hopeful. Unlike Leonard, he also happened to be broke. Ready to go right to work. Seizing upon my blooming sense of hopefulness about the Back Forty, he immediately negotiated an exchange with me—planting trees for underwriting the expense of one of his projects. That sounded fine. Artists are adept in the barter system. My friend, because of his professional connections, bought a half dozen trees, at a greatly discounted price, at a nursery hundreds of miles away where he lived. He then finagled the nursery—with vague promises of future work and pointed remembrances of works past (and more vague references to unlimited budgets and good taste in the offing)—into delivering the trees, a great distance, on a flatbed, and helping him plant them. He quickly located a few extra Helpful Men as well.

Naturally, as soon as the Artist got to work, the neighbor with the broken-down VW bus in the driveway showed up, hysterically demanding to see work permits. We had none; who needed permits to plant trees? Soon after, the police arrived. The neighbor had called them, complaining violently, certain that I was sneaking in another house between us and violating every building code in the books. The police looked around, shrugged the scene up to suburban neighborliness, and left.

They went to work. So did I. In one dervishy day, the crew dug holes and planted and staked all the trees. I came home to find the far end of the yard dotted with new life. The effect was breathtaking. Where there had been only sad, dying trees, there was now a little crowd of healthy green youngsters clamoring for water.

The Artist had blasted through the rock of my resistance. I had wholeheartedly accepted the idea that my garden was "impossible," shrunk my prospects for it, and avoided getting started.

"Let me tell you a story," he said, knocking back his third tequila. Oh, did I forget to mention how helpful a drink is, every now and again, to an artist planting trees? "Let me tell you why you should call me next time you feel defeated.

"A man is walking down a trail, and he falls into a deep hole. He hollers for help. A minister comes by. 'I'll pray for you,' he says. A few days go by, nothing happens. The man is getting hungry and lonely down in his hole. A hiker comes by, hears the man moaning, and, peering over the edge, yells down that he doesn't have the proper equipment to get him out. A few more days pass, the man is in despair. A third guy hears his cries and says, 'Don't worry, I'll help you.' And he jumps into the hole. 'You idiot!' The first man is furious. 'I thought you were going to help me. How could you be so stupid? Now we are both at the bottom of the hole.' 'I thought you might need some company,' said the other man gently. 'And I know the way out.'"

I suppose you might say that the Artist had also established the "bones" of the garden, but if so, they would soon enough need breaking and resetting. Garden designers are always talking about the bones of good design, how they have to be thoughtfully considered, carefully established. In

the case of my garden, the consideration was going to have to happen after the bones went in—and that was what I was doing during the Winter of Last Daydreams: mentally moving trees around. They had all been planted too fast, because I had caught the Artist in a compliant, distracted moment, and because I had ceded all control to him. What's the point of a garden if it doesn't look the way you see it? I spent the next few months thinking about what to rearrange and transplant. But at least, thanks to the Artist, I had broken the curse of the rocky soil. I had gotten over the idea that my plot of land was untillable. I had learned that you can make a garden anywhere.

Friends can nudge you out of torpor, if they come along at the right time. The Artist taught me a fundamental—and joyous—truth of gardening: nothing is impossible, and the only limitations on what you can do are your will and your imagination.

# TEN

# THE THRESHOLD OF SAFETY

*"Those green-rob'd senators of mighty woods,*
*Tall oaks, branch-charmed by the earnest stars,*
*Dream, and so dream all night without a stir."*
—John Keats
"Hyperion: A Fragment, Book 1"

"Dogwoods live at the threshold of safety," Mr. D'Ambrosio was saying. The Winter of Last Daydreams had come to a rude end. As a premonitory flush of warmth was washing over us, the plant pathologist had arrived to pay his call on my garden. I had been dreading his visit, and when he parked his car in the street below, I watched from my bedroom window, wary of someone whose eye was trained on sickness. He had picked his way up the pocked and pitted

driveway, using a stainless steel cane, turned up the narrow, mossy brick path that was almost overrun with azaleas, and stopped, standing, looking out over the Old Garden, with his back to the house. I met him, reluctantly, at the front door.

"What a spot," he had said the moment we shook hands. His eyes were twinkling. He was about my height, and seemed to be in his sixties. He had gravity and an eccentric air combined. "What a beautiful spot. This place is gorgeous. What a magnificent stand of sassafras. Indigenous, you know."

My defenses melted away. No lectures about curb appeal from this one. He understood struggling beauty.

We walked around to the back of the garden together. His helpers had arrived, in a large truck, moments ahead of him, and I had shown them the oak tree in question, whose decay we were meant to be investigating. They were having difficulty getting a rope into the lowest limb, which was very high off the ground.

While they had gone to get a ladder, Mr. D'Ambrosio had begun poking around at the other trees. He was rhapsodic about the dogwoods. I lose my heart to anyone who carries on about trees. I could already feel it slipping its moorings. What could be more poignant, more riveting, than a beautiful creature living at the threshold of safety?

"The threshold of safety," he repeated for emphasis. "Now, what that means is the dogwoods come out of winter with very little fuel left in the tank. They produce flowers before the leaves come out in May. You know how the song goes, 'April showers, May flowers'? Well, we don't have April showers anymore." Mr. D'Ambrosio patted a pack of cigarettes in his shirt pocket, thought better of it, ran a hand through his graying hair, and went on. It was true we hadn't had April's showers, and neither May's nor June's were to come that year. We had settled into a deep and damaging drought.

"Our climate is changing. We have May showers now. There is no longer sunshine in May. The dogwood is blooming before the green leaves come out. There is very little photosynthesis happening, with no leaves. You remember photosynthesis, young lady?"

I remembered it, thankfully.

"You see, the twigs of a dogwood are green. They do what little photosynthesizing the tree can do in the spring. When there is too much rain while the tree is blooming, the tree cannot feed itself adequately. The tree cannot refuel. It becomes weak, and the casual fungi take over. They become pathogens. That is living at the threshold of safety."

I was a goner. I was ready to sit at Mr. D'Ambrosio's feet all day, learning about trees, moved by his tender concern, his understanding of the poor dogwood's vulnerability, how it gave of itself, risking life and limb, to herald the spring.

"We're straining things, here on earth," Mr. D'Ambrosio went on. "You know the difference between stressing and straining?"

Not really.

"Stress, you pull a coil of wire apart, it springs back together. Strain, you pull it out, it never goes back. You've gone too far. We are *straining* our trees."

I could definitely understand the difference. It was the same thing with muscles, and friendships. A person could disappear and return, leave you and come back, only so many times before the heartstrings lost the resilience love needs to thrive. It isn't that you don't care anymore, it's that you give out. It isn't a mystery, it happens right under your nose in the region of the heart. Were my trees giving out? While the helpers were leaning an enormous extension ladder against the tree, and finally getting their thick line looped around a high branch, Mr. D'Ambrosio had gone around to the back of the dogwood and was poking at the base, pulling back ivy and dirt.

"Uh-oh," he said. "Trouble at the top means trouble at the bottom." The leaves at the crown, he pointed out, off one branch at the back, were very thin. The branch was dying. He raised his metal cane. It had an arching handle and came to a long, thin, tapered point; about a foot of the end of it had been trenched.

"Do you need that to walk with?" I asked.

"I need it to probe my trees," he said. "I walk just fine. See the base of this tree back here? See how there is no flare to it when it reaches the ground? That is not normal. Something is wrong with this dogwood. Could be a fungus. Could be a virus. Strained. I don't know what to do about it. You ought to think about planting a new tree now. I give this dogwood two, maybe three more years. So you plant the new tree now, and by the time this one dies, the new one will be established. You know the old rule about planting trees? No? It takes three years. 'First year it sleeps, then it creeps, then it leaps.' Get ready now, young lady."

As I was preparing to break down over this news, there was a shout from up in the oak. We looked up in time to see the helper stick his probe into the hole, wiggle it around, and then pull it out. Even from the ground I could see the black, rotted wood, dark against the steel probe, that filled its trenched end.

"It's bad," said Mr. D'Ambrosio. "Call me Bob."

The helper poked around in the hole some more.

"There is severe decay in there. I can see from here."

The helper parlayed down the side of the tree and walked

over to us, his hands cupped. In his palm was curled a fat, white grub, the length and thickness of my thumb. I shuddered. The larval creature, so white it seemed lunar, was nearly glowing against the black rot; it, the grub, had never seen the light of day. It was so fat and complacent that it made no move to wriggle free of its captor. It just lay there. Digesting my tree.

The grub was significant. It meant that squirrels were not living in the tree—they would have eaten the grubs. Which meant that the decay was so profound that the hole inside was too big for even a squirrel to navigate comfortably.

Mr. D'Ambrosio turned his attention from the grub back to me. "How do you feel about this tree?"

Tears sprang into my eyes.

"I see."

We stood silently for a moment. I could think of nothing to say. As a tear rolled down my cheek, Mr. D'Ambrosio began to speak.

"I'll tell you what I am going to do," he said. "I'll bring you a double bloodroot. From my garden. Do you know about bloodroots? Tiny little things. You break their roots, blood comes out. Indians used to go into the forests and find them, and if a man and a woman were courting, they would break open a root and stain their palms red. If they woke the next morning and their palms were still red, they would know they were meant for each other. Or maybe it was an aphrodisiac, and it made them want each other.

"Isn't that a nice story? I bought a double-flowering bloodroot twenty years ago, this big"—he marked off half of his index finger—"and it cost me twenty-five bucks. That's a lot for a little plant. But the thing has multiplied and multiplied. It just keeps spreading. We'll plant it in a nice shady

spot here, near the oak tree, and in the spring, you'll see flowers like you've never seen in your life. It's a double, they look
like tiny peonies. All ruffles. A petticoat. Gorgeous. You'll be
so happy."

I looked at him, dumbstruck. Here we were talking about
the possibility of losing an oak that was more than a hundred
years old, my pride and joy, and something I had clearly not
taken care of properly—oh, the failure, the guilt—and he was
talking about a flower the size of my finger.

But the tree doctor's gardenside manner worked. I
cheered up.

We continued our stroll around the garden together.

"I love this place," he said. "Just beautiful. Those sassafras
are amazing. Easily a hundred years old. You don't see that
too often."

The stand of sassafras was notable. They were the fastest-
growing trees I had ever seen, easily climbing to fifteen feet in
a few years. Every spring dozens of suckers sprang up out of
the ground. They were impossible to pull up, so deep were the
taproots. The trees had unusual lobed leaves—they came in
three different shapes, on a single tree, the nicest ones looking
like left- and right-handed mittens.

"Uh-oh. What's happening with that one? Why is it so
thin on top? See how there are no more leaves on most of the
branches? It's dying."

He began to poke the base of the sassafras with his probe.
He pointed out the base of the trunk, how it, too, was not flaring properly all the way around. A few more pokes, and then
he banged against the tree. I flinched. Some bark came off.
There was a hollow sound.

"We will have to find out what is wrong here. Have you
had problems with these trees?"

I remembered that a neighboring tree had come down a year earlier.

"And the guys who removed it, what did they tell you? Did they tell you what was wrong with it? No, probably not. They just told you it was dead, and it had to be removed. Which you knew. That's the problem with most of these tree guys. They're just removers of trees. Their attitude is, the tree is alive or it is dead. There's nothing you can do, just get rid of it."

He was right, of course. I had been told, vaguely, there was probably some bug, or old age, the tree was dead, it would fall on the house in the next storm, three hundred bucks to take it down. That is the worst, most abstract kind of money to spend, worse than spending money on the roof or the furnace—the money it takes to have things carted away.

Mr. D'Ambrosio—Bob—was digging a trench across the front of the roots of the sassafras with one of his helpers. They got about four inches deep when he pounced on yet another squishy, large white bug, and, clutching it between a thumb and a finger, he held it up for my inspection. This one had legs, several of them, and they were all sawing frantically at the air.

"These bugs are chewing away the roots of your trees." He pointed out the tunnels that were going from one tree to another. "I'll have to take this back to the lab and analyze it, to see what to do. We'll kill the bugs, or we'll strengthen the tree, I don't know yet. On the other hand, you could have a drainage problem."

This was becoming a nightmare of a garden visit. We walked back to the oak.

"I won't tell you to take it down now. Not now. We are going to put window screen and chicken wire in the opening.

And mothballs. That way the squirrels can't get in, and the bugs can't get out when they hatch. They'll die. That's fine. We don't want them. I'm going to prune all the upward growth, take out a lot of branches so the wind will go through, not against. And we'll keep an eye on it. See how it goes. Don't worry. I'll be back next week. We'll get to work immediately."

He explained that he would make scientific calculations of the degree of decay relative to the mass of the tree, developing a threshold to determine the degree of hazard, using mechanics of solids formulae—never mind, never mind, he had a paper from a scientific journal that would clarify the whole process, and he would send me a copy.

In a gesture of good intention, he left his line looped around the branch, the ends tied into a bundle, dangling high up against the tree.

The next day I received a fax from Mr. D'Ambrosio spelling out his rates. It was addressed to me at the office, re: "your haven," and in it he promised to treat the "astounding" garden "as if it were mine." That was very reassuring. I felt even better when he did not show up the following week. Everything seemed less dire.

The scientific paper was also faxed. "Welcome to my world," Bob had written across the top. A world in which people were trying to "standardize hazard tree assessment." I felt as if I were tottering at the end of a very weak limb, myself. "Bartlett's formula is strength loss = $(d^3+R(D^3-d^3))/D^3 * 100$, where $D$ and $d$ are as above, and $R$ is the ratio of cavity opening to stem circumference . . ." My stomach turned. Luckily, this was "an art as much as a science," I read, and "because trees are individuals, it is impossible to create a 'one size fits all' management plan." I was grasping at twigs, if not straw. I would simply have to wait for Bob's customized diagnosis.

Since then, whenever the wind blows, I look anxiously up into the canopy of the oak tree. Then my eye follows the trunk down to its perfect flare at the ground, and I imagine the lacy bit of double bloodroot that will one day be flowering profusely at its base. How deeply entwined are the roots of beginnings and endings. What an improbable trade—the fate of a tree for the start of a friendship.

plugged it in, and showed me how to pull the lever down and squeeze the handles together to get the mower going. I had never used a power mower before, and was very excited. So was he. For the first time, he offered to help. He would be glad to mow the lawn. So he did. I trailed nervously along behind, asking him to be very careful, begging for a turn. The next week, I could have all the turns I wanted. The lawn mower was no longer fun. It was helping.

But it gave me an idea. Gadgets. The fire truck wasn't so deranged an association. After all, the Boys, like most children, had always thought of their garden as a place to play. The idea of working in a garden (as that is what helping means) was an unfamiliar, unfathomable concept. I was speaking a foreign language. I would have to figure out how to get them to help by playing. My older son was beyond my reach; he was, however, polite enough to take a spin with the mower once or twice more during his last summer before college. (I could see that this had the appeal of creating a moment of nostalgia; he could feel like the teens in old movies who actually earned money mowing lawns, so that they could take girls out on dates, and he could one day look back on a time when he had mowed lawns.) That was the limit. But the younger one had revealed a soft spot, a penchant for playing with tools and equipment. I walked through the local hardware store, searching for gadgets that might prove to be useful—and while I'm on the subject, a word about garden tools: they have become too fancy, ever since it became fashionable for socialites to pretend that they did the gardening. They are overdesigned, too persnickety, too high-maintenance. The tools, not the socialites. (I think.) Some of them even wear fashion designer labels; they are much too expensive.

It is a fact of gardening that the earth will swallow up the fork or the snippers within two minutes of your putting them down to turn to a patch of weeds; if they are brightly colored (forget those chic dark green things) you stand a better chance of finding them, in a year or two, but tools ought not to be such an investment that you feel you must reallocate your assets when they are lost. There is no need to be fetishistic about a trowel—unless, of course, it works perfectly and feels superbly balanced in your hand. You should carry that around in your pocket.

Hardware stores still sell the basic, old-fashioned stuff. I went home with an extension pruner. It had a long handle, about four feet, that telescoped to about seven feet. It had a mechanism that you squeezed with your hand, and the dragon head of a clipper, at the other end, would dramatically snap its jaws and chomp through a branch. It was a very appealing tool. I propped it up in the corner of the kitchen and didn't say a word about it. The Boys circled it warily, taking the long way around to retrieve Pop-Tarts from the pantry. A few days later, during breakfast, Theo asked me about it. I told him that he was forbidden to use it under any circumstance; it was too dangerous, and besides, he didn't know what to lop off.

"You can show me, Mom."

I love reverse psychology. It is so straightforward and has such a long reach. But it only works when the suckers are green. We went into the garden. I set up a small ladder for Theo so that he could feel even taller, and pointed out all the dead branches on the old hydrangea bush. The ones with no green stuff on them, I explained, leaving nothing to chance. With many warnings to be careful, that he was working with a serious piece of equipment, I went inside. Theo went to work.

Within an hour the ground was littered with dead wood. Theo was also on the ground, lying on his back, dazed, looking for all the world like a battle-weary little knight, his shining lance resting by his side.

My hero. He helped.

TWELVE

# MY HEDGE FUND

"On the way

"we passed a long row
of elms. She looked at them
awhile out of
the ambulance window and said,

"What are all those
Fuzzy-looking things out there?
Trees? Well, I'm tired
of them and rolled her head away."
—William Carlos Williams
"The Last Words
of My English Grandmother"

One year I was too tired to cut back the sassafras sprouts that were colonizing the front yard. Too tired to prune the stray azalea branches, clean out the thickets of deadwood. Azalea is patient; the older it is, the more placid it becomes, and it will wait a long time for refurbishing. A sassafras sprout is frantic. It twists and angles rakishly toward a break in the canopy, desperate for whatever light it can get, growing so rapidly that it is at first alarming. Like wisteria, sassafras feels like a fairy-tale plant, the sort of thing that will wrap itself around you if you sit too long, or wall you off from the world.

The sprouts shot up, and I let them go, and within a year they were two or three feet tall. Fall came, the trees turned brilliant shades of red, yellow, and orange, lost their mitteny leaves, and as the wet winter weather set in and the leaves began to rot, the front yard was suffused with the sweet smell of root beer. The sprouts became vulnerably bare, thin sticks, and I figured that was the end of it; the cold would kill them off for me. Spring came around, the sticks were spiked with little white flowers, and they galloped up, headed for a gangly adolescence. Within the summer they were ten or eleven feet tall. Fearing that they would crowd out the old azaleas, I took a large pruner to the sprouts in the middle of the yard.

But while I was in there hacking away, I got the idea that I liked the way the sprouts at the edge of the garden were growing. They were ranked so thickly that they had created a low hedge across the front. The hedge completely hid the house, and me in the azaleas, from the street, and hid the street—and the cars, and the neon lights of the main shopping strip, and everything else—from me. Had I tried, I would not have been able to establish such a dense planting in such a shady spot; improbably, the sprouts were growing out of a rubble of rocks, covered with ivy and honeysuckle, that passed for a stone wall holding up the front of the yard—well, I suppose it must have once been what is called a thrown dry wall, but it looked like it had thrown itself out. The hedge was an unforetold bit of luck. I decided to bank my sassafras.

For once it seemed that lassitude would serve the garden well. You cannot buy sassafras at a nursery; it is very difficult to transplant. Its spread depends on its own pluck in sending suckers out from a dense crochet of roots. It is also a prolific seeder, when it needs to be. Sassafras must have been a great survivor in the wild. It is drought tolerant, and native to North America. There are nearly a hundred medicinal uses of sassafras to be found in the lore of Native Americans— infusions to kill parasitic worms, to treat syphilis, colds, measles; sassafras tea is still consumed in the Appalachians. In Louisiana, filé powder, made from young spring sassafras leaves, dried and pulverized, is used to thicken gumbo. The bark of the older trunks, which was all I could see of the trees out the windows of my first floor, was dark and deeply furrowed; whenever a delivery truck, trying to navigate the deep ruts in the driveway, scraped a tree, the inner bark that was exposed was an unusual salmon brown.

Sassafras wood was once used for bedsteads, in the belief that the spicy fragrance would repel evil spirits (and insects). I began to hoard my sassafras sprouts, coaxing them along— not that they needed my help—hoping to make a wall of them across the front of my house to ward off every kind of trouble I could imagine. And I can always imagine a lot.

The rapid enclosure of the wall began to inspire fantasies of being a modern-day princess, hidden away deep in the woods, sleeping the sleep of the forsaken. Just waiting, in my garden, to be found by a prince wandering in off the sidewalk, etc., etc., and etc. Let it not be denied that a garden can bring out the flake in the best of us.

Another year went by. Things were a little out of control. The Boys were not impressed by the hedge fund. "You don't have to walk to school past that mess every day, Mom," said Alex. The younger one was more direct. "It looks like a haunted house, Mom," he said one evening. Then he noticed that that didn't bother me in the least. The child is fast. "It looks like a crazy person lives here, Mom. An old, nutty lady who is too old to garden." Hmm. The sprouts were now small trees, easily fifteen feet tall, but the green wall had thinned out at the bottom. These trees only wanted to grow in one direction: up. And something was going wrong in the front of the garden. The sassafras hedge had become so thick that the rhododendrons and the azaleas were not getting enough light. The dainty, cascading leaves of the andromeda (which, by the way, is often championed as the only shrub the deer will not eat) were covered with black scale. The skimmia had turned ghostly pale with spots; the elegant mountain laurel, already leggy, was struggling with its own rash of black blemishes. Only the aucuba japonica was thriving. No refreshing breezes were getting through the wall of saplings. The damp, dark airlessness of the front yard was stifling all the plants, making them vulnerable to blights and viruses. I was finally learning the usefulness of the wind in dispersing molds and vapors. There is a reason to get things moving, even the dust. Like all things of value that are hoarded, my fund of sassafras was misguided. I may have been trying to keep trouble out, but all I was doing was keeping it in.

I went to work, one morning, thinning out the wall. I decided to keep a few of the saplings, the straightest ones with the most promise of one day becoming vigorous trees. I was providing for the next generation of the front garden; unfortunately, most of the saplings were growing in the wrong places, likely to topple off their rocky embankment, within a few years, onto the neighborhood's telephone wires. Within ten minutes I was cursing my stupidity in having let the sprouts go so long. What would have been an easy task years earlier had become a vexing chore. The trunks had thickened and grown tough. I could feel my thumb cramping with tendonitis. Even my largest loppers—the ones that were nearly too heavy for me to hold up—couldn't get around many of them; I had to resort to my pruning saw. Slow work. I began to get sloppy, cutting the trees off in their softer middles, planning to return later, when I had recovered my strength, to saw them at the ground.

Weeks later, when the afternoon light was coming through the tree trunks, and breezes were once again graciously circulating through the shrubs, and I could see modern-day princes, and my neighbors, passing by on the sidewalk, I began to wish I had thought of leaving all those amputated trunks standing, and somehow, like the colonial settlers once did, weaving them into a wattle fence across the front of the garden. I felt exposed. Maybe new sprouts would come back next year. I had already forgotten the only dividend I had drawn from that bank of sassafras—there is no hedge against trouble.

THIRTEEN

# A NEW DRIVEWAY

*"... Change*
*Makes every person strange."*
—Mark Van Doren
"I Hear the House Is Gone"

The only person who had ever been gracious about my old driveway was the True Love. He used to call me, from his car on the way over to my house, to tell me he was about a half hour away, and this I knew meant that he was at the bottom of the driveway, preparing for the last leg of the journey. All twenty yards of it. A rough and perilous journey it was, made worse after the fall of the wall, when the rushing river that spilled off the neighbor's yard came gushing down my already crumbling drive. This happened every time it rained, and we had had a wet spring. The resulting erosion had a certain domestic magnificence. There is always that tantalizing challenge, buried just beneath the surface of your lassitude, that tempting question: How bad can it get? The driveway had become a series of long trenches, and you had to navigate your car very carefully at the top of the straits in order not to drag the bottom, or worse, become beached. There was a trick to it, but it involved getting the wheels up onto the edge of the woods, and eventually that edge, too, crumbled and made a new furrow. But the drive had been in bad shape for years. I was accustomed to it, and patient with its decline.

When the True Love signaled his arrival, I would venture to the end of the driveway and jump into the car with him, driver's side, of course—and he, being a thoroughly modern man, would have buckets full of lilacs, so the car would be wreathed in perfume. Somehow, what with greetings and kisses and creepings, and much exclaiming over new tufts of moss and new scrapes on the sassafras, new views through the trees and new plastic monuments in the neighbor's yard, new veins and new craters, and new ways of wrapping arms around a person and a steering wheel at the same time, the trip easily lasted twenty minutes. Or so it seemed. And then, of course, there was the time spent at the top of the drive, when the True Love would turn the volume up on "Red Cadillac and a Black Mustache," throw open the car doors, and sweep me into his arms for a jitterbug.

Well, the True Love understood the magnificence of domestic erosion. Altogether too well, I might add.

Everyone else complained about the driveway. The Boys, in their feverish Campaign for Driveway Reform, reported fresh complaints every time their father dropped them off. "You don't feel it, Mom. Your car is higher. Dad scrapes the bottom of his car every time he comes up the driveway," Theo said.

"Your father never was a good driver, boys," I said cheerfully. "Did I ever tell you about the time in Texas when he was stopped for driving the wrong way down a one-way street? Or the time a homeless person was living in his car during the day, while he had it parked in the garage? Your father never even noticed, the car was already such a mess. . . ."

Their father began dropping the Boys off curbside.

My mother, when she came to visit, simply drove up the lawn and parked in a patch of grass. Okay, so sometimes she crushed a few peonies. It was my fault.

I held firm in my refusal to change it. I liked it. Then, late one night, as I was getting out of my car in a ball gown and high heels, I miscalculated my footing, tripped into a ditch, and twisted my ankle. It was too humiliating to tell anyone how I had hurt myself so I did not. One by one, over the next few months, the Boys came home, arms and legs scraped, bleeding and bruised from having tripped into a trench or two.

Time for a new driveway.

I consulted Leonard. He suggested I call the Helpful Man who had built the back wall, as he would know exactly what to do about the drainage problems. But it turned out that when it came to driveways, that builder fell under the supervision of yet another Helpful Man, named Gary, who took over the whole operation. He was the one with the bulldozer. As I learned, in the Helpful Man business, the bulldozer rules. We discussed the type of driveway I wanted, a variation on the sort of concrete LEGO kit that the wall was made of, and then negotiated a price (or rather, I was told and quickly accepted the price, having learned that if I did not, I would soon be bumped from that year's calendar). We had some heated discussions about shaping, and color, and lighting. I could see that, as a Helpful Man, Gary was going to be a handful; this happens, sometimes. They take charge. These are postfeminist men. As far as they are concerned, the only useful thing that came out of that quaint women's rights era was a woman's right to pay a Helpful Man's bills. I felt as if I had entered my own personal prefeminist era: I was entirely dependent on these men. Still, the wonderful side of Helpful Men is that, once you are in their ken, they will come to your rescue at any time. Gary is the only man I know who will come right over on a rainy Labor Day morning because the sump pump is not working properly and the basement is beginning to flood. That's the code. They are on this earth to be helpful. And they care about doing things right.

Gary had definite opinions. He had definite suggestions. He had a really good eye roll. But the fact was, he cared about doing things in a proper fashion. He ran a small general-contracting business with his father, who did all the carpentry work, and sometimes I would see them, around town, working companionably side by side, the father, who was as quiet and retiring as Gary was sociable, buzzing away on a piece of wood on sawhorses set up in someone's yard, the son directing an endless traffic of plumbers, electricians, and bulldozers. Gary knew how to do things. He understood all the dark, rotted places of a house. He understood wires, and water pipes, and sewage lines. He knew how to make things right. He wasn't afraid of anything. He wasn't afraid to stick his fingers down the mysterious holes drilled into the concrete around the top of the drainage system when the basement was flooding.

"These are supposed to be vents to the pipe," he said. "You can see they are completely clogged. The pipes need the air in order to keep flowing. Gee, I wish I could work today. Labor

Day. What a lost day this week. I am so backed up. I got open drains up the street. A mess. I have too much work."

He scooped out some gravel, some mud, some other unidentifiable debris. Sure enough, the drains burbled into action. He made a little channel out of scraps of wood lying around in the basement, for the water to flow, the way children make channels in front of sand castles at the beach. Gary loved to explain things and he was a natural, generous teacher. I wished I could have gathered several friends and sat at his feet—he would have loved that—to be given a drain-by-drain, pipe-by-pipe, toilet-by-toilet tutorial of a suburban house. I was utterly in his thrall. But, he had critiques. He felt the front of my house was too dark.

"Hey. You're gonna have a beautiful driveway here, don't you want to see it at night? And why don't I change those bulbs up there under the eaves for you while I'm here?" But there is too much wattage in gardens these days—people are even lighting the surf in front of their beach houses—and I wanted to keep my little plot on the moon's calendar. Gary backed down, shrugging his shoulders. "Well, it's your yard. Have it your way. Stay in the dark." We went on to settle on a start date—just a week away—excavation days, days to notify the police that I would have to keep my car on the street overnight, and so on. That was the last I heard from anyone for months.

Fine with me. I wasn't in a hurry to destroy my romance about the old driveway. Something about its crumbling condition matched the feel of the garden; it looked to me like a country lane—okay, a short one—though with the chunks of black asphalt, that was stretching things a bit. Still, changing the driveway made me nervous. It seemed to be such an important part of the garden; it was how you arrived, it set the mood, the expectation. It was the way you left, the last thing you saw. The driveway is the beginning and the end of most suburban gardens. My driveway was clearly not afraid of growing old (like I was); it let the world know it was careworn, but still bearing up.

The months wheeled around to the time of my son's graduation from high school. I had organized a luncheon for friends and family after the ceremony; a few days before the party, I came home from work to find, parked in what that morning had been the driveway, a bulldozer, a deep pit, many huge boulders, no men. The whole thing was cordoned off with a yellow banner marked DANGER DANGER DANGER. The men did not return for a few days, I had fantasies of working the bulldozer myself, and then Gary reappeared, the day before the graduation party, to tell me that the concrete mixer was arriving soon, and while the end of the drive and new sidewalks were being poured, no one was to cross its threshold.

"Fine," I said. "I'm glad you're starting. But high school graduation is tomorrow, I am throwing a big party, and that is the only day you can't pour cement. People have to be able to get to the party. My parents are coming. They can't climb over rocks. Okay?"

"Don't worry. Concrete trucks wouldn't come on Saturday. No one does anything on Saturday. Everything will be fine. This the only way to the house?" said Gary, eyeing the woods dubiously. "No front path?"

"There is a front path. That old brick walk that starts halfway up the drive."

"That? We gotta rip that up. Drainage has to go under there. Don't you want a new path, anyway? That one's a mess, all uneven."

I assured Gary that I did not want a new walk, that if I

PATHS OF DESIRE · 161

could have afforded to I would have paved the entire drive in old brick, as the original owners of the house had done (as we discovered in the course of the bulldozer's excavations). And that under no circumstances should the path be ripped up. The drainage could go somewhere else.

"Somewhere else? Somewhere else? No. The front yard is perfect, all those trees, those bushes. A lot of water comes out those pipes, you know. We gotta hide it somewhere."

After much haggling, Gary and I finally agreed on an alternate course for the mighty waters, down the other side of the driveway and out into a dry well at the front.

The night before Alex's graduation, I woke up at four in the morning, began crying at 4:05—*my baby, don't leave me*—and did not stop until 9:45, fifteen minutes before the ceremony began. I was in no condition, then, to run into the cement mixer at the bottom of the driveway. All the Helpful Men were there, of course, along with some I had never seen before. All working on a Saturday for the first time in the history of Helpful Men. They are like moths to a flame when it comes to heavy equipment. The blasted-out sidewalk had been squared off; cement was gushing into the molds. I didn't even stop. I clambered through the trees, scrambled down some rocks, and went to the high school. Luckily, I was out of tears.

Three hours later, when sixteen of us came back to the house for lunch, the Helpful Men were gone. The wet cement, raked as meticulously as a Japanese Zen garden, was cordoned off. Gary had built a steep ramp up the front and a lovely little path of plywood zigzagging through the trees to the dry part of the drive. The Boys exchanged significant glances. While we were at lunch, every child at the party snuck down the drive to carve his or her initials into the sidewalk; the youngest ones, who had more trouble with spelling, had to try two or three times to get it right. We all know that wet cement is to children what heavy equipment is to Helpful Men.

Gary was outraged, the next day. "There don't seem to be so many kids in this neighborhood," he said, eyeing the trees suspiciously, as if the children might have sprung from them. "Look at all those scribbles." The wall builder was beside himself: "That cement was perfect. Just perfect." Peering down at everyone's handiwork, I claimed ignorance of the culprits, though their identities were staring us in the face. "Well, it's your driveway," said Gary. I suppose everyone got some sort of revenge on everyone else, and I got a lovely souvenir of graduation day.

Not so fast.

The following Monday, I came home from work to find the driveway smooth, tamped down, and ready for the laying of the blocks. Every trace of the twenty-minute drive had been erased. But the front yard looked strange, somehow. By the time I had figured out what it was, Gary had arrived in his truck.

"Yeah, I tossed a coupla rocks in there," he said.

"In my garden? You put boulders in the garden?"

"What-am-I-gonna-do-with-'em? I can't take them to the dump. They don't want them. They charge extra to take rocks. They moan and groan when you pull up with a truck full of rocks. What-am-I-gonna-do-with-'em? Nobody wants your rocks."

"So you put them in my garden?"

There were four huge boulders clumped awkwardly among the azaleas; one of them had half a bush pinned under it.

"Yeah, in there. In the trees, where all those weeds are."

"Weeds? Weeds? Those aren't weeds, Gary. Those are plants. Plants I put there. Plants that have been there a hundred years. Plants that I weed, you know? I work hard in there. I remove the weeds from the plants. There aren't any weeds in there. There's pachysandra, and vinca, and ivy, and Solomon's seal, and azalea, old azalea, and—"

"Yeah, I ran a nursery once. I know azaleas."

"And why does that azalea look so funny? Why is it tilting?"

"That's where we ran the drainpipe. Under the azalea. We had to move it a bit—"

"You said you weren't going to put the pipe on that side. We agreed. Remember? And you tore up the path!"

"Listen. We'll put the path back. It'll look just like new. I mean old. Like you like it. The azalea will be fine. I had a nursery once. I know azaleas. I can get you one just as big and fat as that one, if anything happens. But nothing is gonna happen. Everything will be fine—"

"Why are men always telling me everything will be fine? Everything is not fine!"

"Hey, you worry too much about this stuff. Leave it to me. I'll take care of it. You worry too much about ivy. Trust me. It'll grow back. I've seen it."

He was right, everything was fine. I got him to move a few of the boulders, I pruned the wounded azalea, the brick walk was put back unevenly, and the driveway was a thing of beauty.

Too beautiful. I was in shock. It looked new. It looked different. It looked smooth. It looked swanky. It looked so fancy you could throw a cocktail party on it. The worst of it was, it looked inviting. My garden was meant to be entered by slow degree, and the old driveway had set the pace. I would have to invent other distractions along the way. The new driveway was going to cause fresh trouble, I could tell.

The FedEx man was complimentary. The UPS man whistled. The postman said he might even start using the driveway, instead of cutting through the trees. Everyone came to see the new driveway—my sister, my parents, my girlfriends (the Three Graces, also known as the Tribunal, who pronounced a steely hope that this development might keep the True Love out of my garden for the rest of time, as they had one by one turned against him due to his increasingly unreliable presence—or reliable absence).

The graduate was thrilled. He is the sort of child who appreciates order. My youngest, who appreciates disorder, came home from camp; his father, effusively complimenting Theo on the new driveway, deposited him and his large, heavy trunk right in the middle of it. Theo rang the bell, and by the time I got to the door he was unpacking the trunk, spreading his clothes and crafts out on the driveway as if it were the floor of his room. He set up a little display of his prizes. He scattered his filthy clothes around to get some fresh air. He retrieved his folded camping chair from the bottom of the trunk, opened it up, sat in it, and began to rock. He had the right idea. I leaned against the stairs to the side door. We settled in for a nice, long visit, on the driveway; it could have been a new patio. Theo recounted the horrors of summer camp. From the new driveway, I sat and gazed into the other-side-neighbor's oak. From the new driveway, I noticed a blackened pit in the middle of the trunk, and watched as squirrels scurried up and disappeared into the hole. From the new driveway, I realized I had no intention of telling the neighbor about the hole in his oak. I had been happier without the knowledge of rot in *my* Garden of Eden.

My father called to check up on the progress, and I began to whine. *The new driveway, it looks new, it looks different, it looks fancy, it isn't the same,* and on and on. My father listened patiently, somewhat used to me by now.

"It looks like the runway of a small airport!" I said. "All that's missing is a sign that says 'Land Here! Come visit! Welcome!'"

"Well, darling," he said sensibly. "Maybe that's not such a bad message."

# FOURTEEN

# THE LONG AND WINDING PATH

*"The garden flew round with the angel,*
*The angel flew round with the clouds,*
*And the clouds flew round and the clouds flew round*
*And the clouds flew round with the clouds.*

*". . . that things go round and again go round*
*Has rather a classical sound."*

—Wallace Stevens
"The Pleasures
of Merely Circulating"

I have shelves full of earmarked garden books. They brim with gorgeous pictures of plant combinations, suggestions for the layout of flower beds, blueprints for the shaping of terraces. For years, I piled nursery catalogs into bed with me during the winter months, and, alternating chapters with whatever novel I happened to be reading, I ripped and folded my way through the paper storefronts. I long to reproduce something I clipped from a story about an English garden: a double row of lavender flanking a long, thick bed of crimson peonies. What a striking effect. Or that tall stand of hydrangea backed against an old brick wall in a Long Island garden, its blooms a tumbling riot of turquoise and garnets, pruned high enough off the ground to make room at its feet for a calming mass of the dark, sedate, thick-leaved bergenia. I want mullein tucked into every cranny of the stone wall I will never build, preferably "Album" *Verbascum chaixii.*

The list of things I wish I could grow but never will is endless; the sun is never the right kind of sun; I don't have the proper pH content in my soil; the wind is predominantly from the southwest, and is parching, and carries with it the noxious fumes of the cars speeding up the nearby parkway; the rainfall is unpredictable. I have no space for flanking rows, and not enough sunlight hours in which to properly groom mounds of lavender into plump spheres. My plants grow and lean and crane in one direction—west—by the end of the day; undernourished, they crave the last rays of the evening. I could never restrain myself to a choice of two plants for the brightest bed; my sort of gardening involves polygamous devotion. Useful suggestions and pretty pictures are an enormous inspirational resource, and of limited practical value. Just as you cannot select a paint color for your dining room because you like the way it looked when you sat at someone else's table, so you cannot choose to plant your garden by another person's beds. You can only get a yen for something. After that, what you can do depends on the play of your own light. Soil is amendable, water taps turn on and off, but sunbeams and breezes slip through your fingers.

The suburban gardener makes a choice, by planting trees. There is not room for a distant grove. The trees will cast shadows close to the house; those shadows soon turn into deep pools of shade. I had a choice. Many of my trees had died and I could have given up on the idea of wooded land; when the Winter of Last Daydreams was over, and it came time to plant, I chose trees, again. The rest of my garden would have to live in the shade of my first love. I would plant a shade garden. And I would have to do my best with the patches of dappled sunlight that would come of diligent pruning.

Along with trees, there was another feature I chose. Curves. Chose? Or was forced to? (Or is there a difference? Choices so often seem to be the decisions we make when forced.) Shelves of granite ran along the side of the house; years of rain had washed away the topsoil and left much of the stone exposed. Those stony expanses were joined by the implacable presence of boulders so large that the builder of a hundred years ago simply left them uncovered wherever they chanced to lie. Over the years more stone heaved up from the ground, as the soil settled around it. I suppose if I had had a truly geometric turn of mind, I could have blasted things out, or deepened the grade of the soil, to make room for rectangular beds. As it was, there could be no strict plan for the placing of trees, or even shrubbery, for I never knew when my spade would ring against rock. I have always wanted to be what I am not: a modernist, a minimalist, a geometrist. Ruthlessly, unerringly disciplined. This is fantasy. Every time I am forced to act, my natural inclinations take me in the opposite direction. To my eye, the gaunt, truculent edges of my oblong suburban plot needed the counterpoint of curved beds to soften and harmonize the yard.

The fact is, I needed a wandering sort of garden.

Two strips of lawn had for years groped their way into the side yard. One ribbon started at the front door and snaked along the front of the house before heading into the side yard, and the other strip started at the kitchen door, ran along the back of the house, and made its way, parallel to the front strip, into the side of the yard. The two strips did not connect; their meeting was interrupted by the square of old flagstone off the side porch. It was generous to call these threadbare carpets a lawn. Grass is not pleasant about shade, and grows wan and petulant near trees. Still, the previous owners had coaxed it along, and the grass had done better as the hemlocks died off and let more sun through. I picked up the effort, and the grass eventually found its way back into the full sun at the far side of the yard, next to the neighbor's driveway full of cars, where it crept over the stony ridges. By the beginning of the Winter of Last Daydreams I did have passable lawns.

I hated them. They weren't appealing, except in a place where my view would have been of a dead battery and old tires. They were full of weeds; they looked as if they had been turned out of a salad bowl. (I once made a valiant effort to weed the lawn, and spent ten hours on my hands and knees plucking and easing thick white taproots from the ground. I must have covered at least eight square feet. A week later, the weeds had returned in triplicate.) To mow the lawns, the crew of wildly incapable men, before I had fired them, had run over the trailing branches of every shrub that dared hang a blossom over the grassy edge. Tree trunks and root knees were continually being chipped and lacerated by the careless mowers, who were in a hurry to scalp the fifty other lawns they would descend upon that day. The trumpet vine you were so carefully training up a fence post? Clipped.

The clematis whose feet needed protection? Whacked. The tendrils of vinca you were coaxing across a bare spot? Oh. That wasn't a weed?

The lawn looked thirsty no matter what the weather; skip a meal, and it began to choke. The only grass that is handsome when parched is the high grass of a meadow, because it is laced with blue cornflower or sunny goldenrod, or the nodding, embossed bone-china, saucer heads of Queen Anne's lace. Firing the lawn crew was the last straw; from the next spring on, I would be the one mowing. So I had to reduce what needed mowing.

The hardest thing to decide was how to resculpt the lawn to create new beds; I knew I wanted more room in which to plant things, but I couldn't see exactly how to get it. For months, I unspooled yards and yards of neon-colored pink, orange, and yellow cord and shaped the outlines for new planting areas on the ground. (The bright nylon cord was the smartest purchase I had ever made, in designing the garden. Not only is it pliant and changeable, and visible from afar, it is also a great tool for communication. How many misunderstandings occur due to the ambiguity of instructions like, "Just cut the border of the bed over there"?) I felt like a child, coloring a bold line around the edge of her picture first—and indeed, that was the way my mother had taught me to use coloring books: edge first, thickly, and smudge in from that border before adding more color inside the lines. The effect was grand; I still swell with the memory of praise heaped on my work by an astonished (as I like to think of her) kindergarten teacher. From then on, I lived by strong, but blurry, lines.

Perhaps, in the way that only a garden can draw out, a childlike sensibility in me began to take over the design of the new beds. Whatever it was, I moved the cording around to my heart's content. Leonard joined in the fun, from time to time, with his own helpful loops. The fact is, even though I didn't want it, I needed professional help. But only a wizard could have peered into my heart and told me what I wanted.

"I dunno, drawings might have been easier. Where'd you get this stuff, anyway?" Leonard would say, holding up a skein of bright pink cord.

As there had been no snow that winter, I had a long time to contemplate my drawings against the hard, brown earth, and I did so, wrapped in blankets, from various chairs moved around in the garden, as well as from my bedroom balcony, the sofa on my porch, and the windows of the living room, which gave out on the side yard. I wound the pink and orange cords around tree trunks, past the sandbox, into the spreading puddles of pachysandra.

When spring came, I tried outlining a small pool that could contain the fountain I longed for. I had always wanted a fountain of my own, since I was a little girl. I never got one, and I had discussed this endlessly with the True Love. He had even taken a couple of turns making fountain shapes with the neon pink cord before he got bored and wandered off. He was making himself scarcer and scarcer that spring, following the pattern of the previous autumn. I had begun to taste fear on his lips. I had my hands full and didn't quite want to see what was coming. I was dimly aware that some bulbs couldn't be forced, but I didn't know what to do about it.

Leonard and I made pink rectangles for the border, orange rectangles for the patio wrapped around the fountain, yellow rectangles for the edging around it—so many rectangles within rectangles that we got tangled up in the cord and it became impossible to see what we were doing.

"You thinking of water plants in here?" Leonard said.

"Lily pads? Papyrus?" Of course, every page of my water garden catalogs was clipped and marked and circled and starred. What about some *Ludwigia repens* (primrose creeper)—when you read garden catalogs, you are immediately thrown into the Latin names—with its little yellow flowers, or the fragrant *Mentha aquatica,* a water mint that bore lilac pink blooms? Or *Cyperus haspan,* a dwarf papyrus whose slender stems were topped with two-inch green pom-poms. Better yet: *Alternanthera reineckii,* aka "Hot Flash" (just what I needed, at this time in my life), with its ruby red leaves. We would have had to dig a pond to contain all the stuff I wanted.

"Fish? Carp? You want carp?" Leonard said, and then quickly thought better of it. "I don't know. Around here, with your raccoons, you might as well open a sushi bar."

In the end Leonard talked me out of the fountain altogether; there would be damage to the roots of the dogwood in digging out the basin, and the maintenance, even in simply keeping the drain and pump free of fallen leaves, would be time-consuming. So I decided that a sprinkler system would be my fountain.

I was tired of years of dragging hoses all over the yard, even though there is almost no garden chore I like better than watering. Get Freudian about it if you must, but there is a real sense of power and satisfaction in watching that life-giving liquid stream out of the nozzle in your hand, redirecting an endless flow into whatever bed you want. Never mind. I could water lavishly, but I began to feel guilty about the waste of water when I absentmindedly left the sprinklers running overnight, flooding the basement and creating bogs in close proximity to deserts. This was especially bad as we were in a drought the likes of which we had not seen in years; watering was severely restricted, and hoses and sprinklers were the least effective way to get the most out of the gallons we were allowed each week.

The hoses presented their own problem. Are they part of the grand obsolescence plan? The metal ends are always getting squashed, though I do not know how. Somewhere along the line, each hose would kink and split. The True Love made me a gift of new connectors for my hoses, with elaborate explanations about slicing rubber and male and female ends—who knew?—but those baubles sat for a year on my dressing table, among my necklaces and brooches, like big, brassy earrings, twinkling in the soft lamplight.

I justified the additional cost of a watering system (not only was I pouring money into holes in the ground, I was now spraying it into the air) by telling myself it was pointless to plant things that I wouldn't be able to kept moist. To tell the truth, my bills were alarmingly high. I was in overdraft. But I couldn't stop; the garden must be the birthplace of the legendary slippery slope. And my idea of balancing a checkbook had become to make sure there were plenty of checks left for the Helpful Men. I would soon be forced to stop; Theo, alarmed that I might run out of money for new skateboards and ramps, was already making helpful suggestions about going on a Money Diet. But in went the sprinkler system. The sprinklers became my fountains. Every once in a while, the thrum of the pipes wakes me at dawn, and I sit on a bench and watch the mist rise up out of the ground, the early sun throwing rainbows through the water; as the geysers spray and wheel across the beds, I listen to the susurration of the jets, and I understand how Louis XIV became obsessive about his canals and fountains at Versailles.

By the end of the winter, I was beginning to have neon-colored hallucinations about what to do with the garden. It made sense to think about my plot of land in four parts; when you have a small yard, you can make it feel bigger by dividing it into even smaller parcels. Somehow, that gives a sense of discovery; moving from one garden area to another expands the horizons. I had to work with: the Old Garden in front; a completely neglected, tiny triangle off the kitchen door that was sliced off from the house by the driveway, but was sunny enough to take lots of plants; the bright, hot New Back Bed, under the new wall, off the kitchen, that I had already taken care of (or so I thought); and the side yard, that Back Forty, on which I was now concentrating most of my attention. (I decided to ignore the Holding Pen altogether; it would continue to be useful as a place to bury mistakes.) It was difficult to see what to do with that forlorn Back Forty; it was the largest and most challenging, with its rocky soil and shade, part of my yard. It needed a muscular design. I decided to divide that side into two parts, and shape the new garden around the few old trees already there. I did not stop to consider the wisdom of hanging the design of an entire garden off one surviving hemlock, three doddering dogwoods, and a wounded oak. I suppose if I had wanted to live in the woods, I would have moved deeper into the country. I didn't. I wanted sidewalks and neighbors close enough by for security. I wanted shops within walking distance. But I also wanted a retreat, a place that could cast a spell of quiet peace. I wanted a domesticated woodland.

The pink and orange cords Leonard and I were so carefully laying down snaked around the trees to make beds that soon grew to contain every wayward boulder in the yard. Then the cords swallowed up the edges of the small flagstone patio off the living room porch. And finally, by the time the first snowdrops had flurried up from the ground in early spring, the cords were drawing all the trees into their embrace. Soon, there would be no lawn left at all. Katharine S. White, an editor, a gardener, and a writer, once wrote that "home would not be home without a lawn"; just in case she was right—as she was about most things—I decided to move the cords around one more time. I preserved, in a new configuration, two ribbons of grassy paths, one in the front part of the garden, and one at the back.

They would be my lawns, and there is one excellent thing about having a lawn in a suburban garden. (In fact, most suburban gardens have as their chief feature a lawn, and all statistics I have ever seen measuring the soaring amounts of time spent gardening include lawn care in their parameters; that is what most gardening is about, in the suburbs. Lawns really say a lot about suburbia, with their complicated balance of display, if not outright ostentation, compulsiveness, and a wastefulness that is a sort of tastefulness. For Olmstead, Sr., who began laying out American suburbs in the 1860s, lawns were almost a political consideration: a lawn ensured that the house was "not far removed from the life of the community." A few trees were necessary, too, judiciously placed to provide enough seclusion to give "suggestions of refined domestic life," which is funny when you think about it: anyone seeing too much of life in a suburban house would be aware that refinement was not exactly its defining feature.)

The most excellent thing about the lawn: it is the only place in the suburban garden to lie flat on your back on the earth. We never do that, we grown-ups. And we're constantly telling the children to get up off the ground. We hardly even lie on our backs in the sand at the beach anymore, what with those low-slung folding chairs and back boards and all manner of bucking up and bracing our bodies. The closest we come, nowadays, is a yoga class, and we only lie flat for a few minutes because we are paying good money to follow instructions.

Flat on your back. Nothing under your head. Arms splayed at your sides. The way babies lie in their cribs. Legs relaxed into the earth, toes falling outward. Grass tickling the back of your neck. Gazing up at the sky—remembering how the clouds once looked like ravening tigers or exotic camels or depleted elephants—gazing up into the canopy of a tree. Your body sinking, in one, connected piece, into the earth. The earth.

Remember weather? Most of us suburban gardeners are office workers. We are in sealed buildings all day long. The only weather we follow is the climate control; we atavistically locate the temperate zones in the heating system, the frigid zones created by the cooling system. You can get to the end of the day and find yourself asking, was it a sunny day? Did it rain? When you lie on your back on your patch of lawn in your suburban garden, you are once again connecting to sun and rain and cool and damp and rich and buggy. You might even get a nap.

A nap would be nice. This suburban gardener, like most of her friends these days, has stretches of sleeplessness, during which fantasies of the garden occupy much of the time. In the Winter of Last Daydreams especially, I thought about the garden so much that it entered my sleeping dreams. I drove past other gardens, I flew over stone walls, I stole people's healthy trees—so it was with great relief, during one of those endless dream journeys, that I could finally pull off the road. But as I tried to park, some force greater than I kept pulling my arm, swerving my car, finally dragging it off the shoulder, parking it right on someone's kempt lawn. What a mess I was making. The force kept pulling—

"Mom. Mom. Wake up."

Why couldn't I get the car off the lawn, and parked properly? Why did I keep pulling the wheel the wrong way?

"Wake up, Mom. Wake up."

Theo.

"Wake up, Auntie Doe. Please."

Hunter, tugging on the other arm. Hunter is an honorary member of the Boys; he is my nephew, and spends time at my house to get real Boytime away from his sisters. When we have Boys' Dinner every Monday night, the sisters are not allowed to put even a toe on my driveway. Hunter often sleeps over.

"Mom. Wake up. The garden is coming into the house. We heard it. Or maybe a mouse. A mouse in the house, in the heating vent. Or someone has come in from the garden. We hear it. Wake up."

"No, boys. There is no mouse. Well, probably there is a mouse in the house. But the garden isn't in the house. Well, I guess it could be. Is it raining?"

I ask you, which is more important, the person who is already asleep, or the person who cannot get to sleep? One has everything to lose, the other nothing. As the Boys were having night terrors—and it seemed like everyone had gardens on their minds late that night; could I have been asking them to help too often that day?—we got up and went downstairs to eat buttered toast, very soothing, and to have a look at the garden in the moonlight. I made sure there were no cars parked on the lawn.

Dreams aside, to help me plan the garden, I tried some fast browsing through the catalogs I had stopped looking at for a few years. But somewhere along the way, the garden brochures had fallen under the sway of marketing gremlins; they seemed out of breath—and out of their minds—under

the strain of inventing clever ways to tempt the hapless gardener. Too clever by half. What self-respecting gardener
would want to identify a display of daylilies to her admirers as
a bank of "Eenie Weenies"? I would hardly think of introducing azaleas called "I'll Be Damned" into my garden.
Could anyone seriously think that a hosta called "Striptease"
was attractive? Or an iris known as "Roaring Jelly"? I could
just picture—and it was not a pretty sight—a clump of iris
called "Hello Darkness" standing knee-deep in a bog, ready to
drown her sorrows. Not in my garden, Old Friend.

I was better off, once spring arrived, wandering through
Leonard's nursery, checking on what was available, double-
checking my understanding of where things might work. It
was interesting to learn what would grow well, nestled in
another's shade, and what needed to stand apart to thrive. I
could never draw my own crude plans on paper; there was too
much unpredictability about the terrain. Besides, except in the
broadest strokes, paper never tells you what you really want to
know—how it will look. No wonder Leonard refused to
make plans. So as soon as the weather lightened up, I strolled
through the nursery, pad in hand, and made my selections.

The day came, very early in the spring, that Leonard and
his crew arrived with a truckload of plants, and we spent hours
placing shrubs, their root balls wrapped in heavy burlap, and
moving the bright cord around some more, and deciding
how the paths connecting the two ribbons of grass would
wend.

I wanted to be able to stroll through my garden, just as I
had strolled through the nursery. I had first laid out my
corded beds so that they butted up against too many obstacles;
I had created a couple of dead ends. There was no way to get
from the front of the garden to the back without going

around again. And while the obstinacy of that sort of path appealed to me at first—this is as far as you go, Buster—I didn't really want to be stopped over and over again. A dead end is of limited value.

It is better, in a garden (as in life, or a love affair), if you always think there is something more. That was when the stepping-stones came into the picture. They would go through the new beds we were planting, like the dotted lines on a map, taking you from one part of the garden to another. The stone paths made the connections between the front and back lawns. The stepping-stones took you all the way to the far edge of the garden, out into the sunny places, but they wouldn't make you stop there, unless you were in a particular mood to scowl upon the neighbor's slovenly ways. The perimeters of the stepping-stones would eventually give me plenty of little places in which to dig little holes for little plants, my favorite kinds—the Irish mosses, the creeping thyme, the ginger, and the mottled, bruised ajuga—the sorts of plants you must bend over and peer at to appreciate. And further, the paths would give me something more to sweep, which is a very satisfying thing to do out-of-doors.

Finally, Leonard announced that it was time to make a commitment, to stop playing with colored cords, to stop moving balled and potted plants around and actually get them into the ground. It was time to carve the shapes of the beds into the earth, and set the stones of the paths into place, and actually plant the plants. Everyone can use a Helpful Man to keep the momentum of reality going.

The matter of visually connecting the Old Garden in front to the new one at the side was our trickiest challenge. The trees planted by the Artist, at the far edge of the yard, were a bit of a hodgepodge, owing, again, to my polygamous nature. I simply cannot go to a nursery without falling hard for any number of things, and I must be forcibly kept from turning my garden into something resembling a yard sale. Or, more politely, a "specimen garden," which is usually a euphemism for a garden with a lack of coherence. I had finally "narrowed" my selection—thinking of the broken-down VW bus that I no longer wanted to see—to evergreens whose needles were a deep, rich shade, like the Norway spruce, and would form a nice backdrop for trees that were a softer blue-green shade, like the *Cedrus atlantica* "Glauca," the Blue Atlas cedar. Some Leyland cypresses were clustered to conceal the old tires. I selected two pairs of hinoki cypresses to stand sentinel at either side of my front and kitchen doors. The trees at the side were only a couple of years old, and some of them were struggling in the rocky soil. They weren't blocking my view of anything, yet, and they looked scraggly by comparison with the thick stand of sassafras and the old rhododendron in the front.

The Old Garden gave us the direction for going forward; we needed to blur the line between front and side by continuing the underplanting of rhododendrons and white azaleas. However, remembering the lesson of the hemlocks, too much of a good thing wiped out by a single scourge, we mixed in some snowball viburnum and laurel and hydrangea as well, shrubs that would add a second, and lower, screen in front of the evergreen trees. We planted peegee hydrangea by the side, to hide the VW bus. We massed the rhododendrons in one large group to one day hide the other neighbor's swing set, though the children would no doubt be in law school by the time the bushes were high enough to screen very much. We also planted a few more fast-growing cedars; not my favorite trees, under most circumstances, but suburban gardens offer devil's choices—plastic playthings versus plasticky trees. There was no possibility of continuing the sassafras in any deliberate way; I would have to depend on the chance that whatever suckers the trees sent up might be well placed.

Still, once the shrubbery was settled into place, there was a "do-si-do-your-partner" effect as the trees exchanged positions from deciduous to evergreen and the shrubs laid down a rhythmic flow. That was the intention, anyway. The reality will not play itself out for years—as is usually the case in a garden.

All danger of frost passed, and we kept going, planting dozens of hosta, and I was careless about mapping what variety went where, because I knew I would never care what their names were; I cared only for the way the colors mixed, and caught what dappled light they could. We planted violet and lavender astilbe, laurels, and all sorts of hydrangea: the oak-leafed *H. quercifolia* (a new crush of mine), peegee, or *H. paniculata "Grandiflora"* (like the ones already throwing off huge bouquets in the older part of the garden), and the smaller *H. macrophylla*. I planted Solomon's seal, trillium, ferns, and, where the garden crept into the sun, dozens of hellebores, another new passion, and echinacea, daylilies, ginger, and vinca under it all.

As soon as planting was over, it was time for transplanting. Leonard graciously rolled his eyes only a bit—what would the job be without the stress?—at my changes of heart.

And finally, the garden was done. No, not done. It will never be done. Already I see things I don't like: combinations of colors that look off, like the golden daylilies too close to the pink astilbe (but did anyone know, tagging the plant, it was going to come up pink?); groups of plants that inadvertently fell into straight lines; clumps that aren't massed in a balanced way and look forlorn. And of course there are way too many bare patches, way too many puddles of mulch showing.

But the Back Forty, too far from my heart to care about, was no more; the side yard was transformed. It had become a garden. The Wandering Garden. And now it was time to ponder the effect, and wonder how it would all look in ten years. Or next spring. Back to sitting around again, but why not? It is one of the pleasanter parts of gardening. This time, though, I had placed a heavy teak chair in the far corner of the yard, out in the shade of the oak and the dogwoods, the corner in which I had spent so many years daydreaming from my aluminum chairs. There was no longer a need to drag lightweight chairs around out there; I had traveled down my paths of desire long enough to find a perfect place to sit still. The armchair was now surrounded by small shrubs and clusters of hosta and Solomon's seal. It was at the end of the back ribbon of lawn on one side, and at the start of a stepping-stone path on the other. It was a place to rest on what could be a long stroll through the garden. The evergreens behind would eventually screen me entirely from the neighbors' view. From that corner, with the old oak standing sentry on one side, and the only surviving (and now thriving) hemlock on the other, I could look over the new beds.

And so there I sat and gazed on my new garden, and gazed into my heart, too, wondering why the True Love had been so absent through the spring planting. I was growing more used to his absence than his presence. But that had been his way— our way. He had been in and out of my life for years, and I had come to think of him as having taken deep root in such a shaded spot that sometimes I could not even find him, but he was impossible to pull up entirely. Perhaps it is not so helpful to think of people as plants. It is only comforting.

One evening, I realized, with a guilty start, that even if the True Love did happen to wander again into my garden, he would not have had a place to sit. A friend well versed in the tricky art of feng shui pointed out that that far corner just happened to be the relationship corner of my plot of land, striking terror in my heart that I may have jinxed everything with my solitary chair. So I dragged another heavy armchair out to the corner, just in case. At least the chairs looked happily companionable. And then I thought, well, if we were out there having a glass of wine together, there would be no place to put the glass down between sips; one Saturday morning soon after, the consignment shop in the next town sent out its seductively magnetic rays, which were always effective in drawing me into a purchase that was just there waiting for me. I drove to the store and, this time, it was a pair of ancient Chinese bronze dragons calling out to me, their heads grinning ferociously at the base, their tails balancing small trays. Into the garden I hauled my dragons, and placed them on either side of the armchairs, and now the entire thing looks very regal and commanding, though perhaps the dragons, with their fierce looks, are a bit intimidating. Too bad. True love is not for the fainthearted.

And one evening, looking at the result of so much dreaming and digging, I suddenly recognized what I had done. I had inadvertently drawn up, out of some deep reservoir of memory, a new garden that captured all the things I had loved best about the first garden I had ever been aware of, a garden I worked in, when I was five years old, side by side with my father.

That garden had been heavily wooded, and full of long and winding paths that actually went somewhere: to a river. Every afternoon, as soon as school was out, I would pick a path to follow—and my father, with me trailing behind to help, had carved out of the sloping woods at least five of them, straight, skinny, curvy, long, short, decorated, and so on. I would pick a path, and, as it came to the end of the woods, I would break into the sunshine and scramble down to the river, where I spent hours crouched on the banks, watching the quick riffle of water over bright pebbles, listening to it cascade over boulders, watching the birds and the fish and the animals that went to the river to bathe or drink. I felt protected by those woods, delighted by the river, proud of having braved the adventure to get there, and always sure that I could find my way home again. Home was at the end of whatever path I chose to follow.

I think it was Faulkner who described two kinds of memory: one that springs from the mind, the other lodged in the body. Perhaps there is a third kind, for some of us: a memory of the ground, some visceral sense of what the earth is supposed to feel like under your feet. Perhaps that is simply a memory of place. We all have it, but it must be selective particularities of a place that are indelible. My new garden was not an exercise in nostalgia. Its design had not been deliberately evocative of my childhood. In fact, had I realized what I was doing before I did it, I am sure I would have resisted the impulse to dig that far back into the past. As it is, I am sure I am the only one who can see the garden this way; even my father would not sense its familiarity. And why would he? His experience of those woods was entirely different from mine. He was an adult. He was digging paths to release the tension of the week's work. He was a Kentucky country boy learning the ways of Northeastern soil. He was making his first home for his new family. What loomed large for me looked small to him. What he did—what we did together—cast one spell on me, another on him; that is how it goes, with gardens, with houses. Like the stream, impossible to step in the same place twice.

And there it was again, a path of desire. This one was ancient, invisible, etched into my heart. The path in my new garden didn't go anywhere, exactly; it looped back on itself so you could stroll it over and over again. You could say it had no end. Still, it was a path. I had planted trees; I had stepping-stones; there were sunny spots and pools of shade; the quartz veins in the bedrock at the far end of the garden sparkled like water in the sun; the lilies waved and winked on the breezes; the whole thing had, somehow, the feel of the garden that had meant the most to me, that had made a gardener of a small child. And the new path got me home, too.

In actuality I would be looking at a lot of mulch for the next few years. I don't really like looking at youthful plantings, but it was impossible for me to spend the money to transplant mature trees and shrubs. It seemed like cheating, somehow. It would be many seasons before the scrawny stems of young ferns dotted about under the hemlock would stand thick and tall, and the strings of vinca plugged in everywhere would cover the ground. So what if my sward of daisies ran the short length of a café curtain? So be it. Plants are easier to move around when they're young and small, and they take better to new surroundings. If you lose a few, it isn't grievous. The only plants breaking my heart in the garden were the old ones.

In any event, most of the time I don't see my garden as it really is.

Of course, it is a suburban garden. That means, in the evening, that the streetlights cast their beams through the sassafras; that the neon lights of the local picture house flicker over; that headlights from the cars passing by in the night swing eerily across my bedroom walls; that what sounds like a rushing river is really traffic on the parkway; that raccoons and possums and skunks will frighten me enough to keep me indoors after dark; that people parking their cars on the street will slam their doors and honk their horns and empty their ashtrays at the edge of the yard; that car alarms will jangle to life of their own accord; that leaf blowers will grind all day, blowing suburbia's topsoil into the gutters; that the aging musician will rev the engine at three in the morning; that someone's little dog, outside at the crack of dawn, will yap shrilly and cut through my sleep; that airplanes shrieking into the sky will make my ears ring; that the long, low wail of the train will scatter my thoughts; that kids prowling through the night will heave their empty beer cans into the azaleas; that my hammock will be stolen from its hooks in the trees; that my *car* might be stolen from the driveway; that I can smell what is cooking on other people's grills; that the windows of the houses all around me are lit up, and I can hear the murmur of adults in conversation at dinner, or the despair of sleepy children at bedtime.

But when I sit in my armchair at twilight, tucked into the coves and eddies of the garden, at the end of a languid stroll over the stepping-stones, listening to the hum and buzz of cicadas and crickets, thrilling yet again to the fireflies, and gazing over the new beds, all that fades away. I am ensorcelled. I see my garden as it will look years from now, when branches have thickened and elongated, saplings grown taller, when shrubs have become mature, ferns clumped and hosta ringed itself round more deeply. I see that the hydrangea that now hangs in the way of the path, asking you to lift its swooping branch out of your way, will someday arch gracefully over your ducking head. I see that the daylilies that now straggle along the walk will one day be dense with golden blossoms, and that I will be able to snip a few off, with so many to spare, and set them in shallow bowls of water through the house, where, true to their names, they will crumple by day's end. And I will do the same thing over again, summer after summer. I see that the clethra will be tall enough to send its opulent fragrance of honey through the library window; that the lilacs will fan across the living room window and I will sit at my piano with the window thrown open, breathing in a heady perfume. The hydrangea will offer up, each fall, its rosy, bronzed bouquets. The mounding sedum will send up dozens of spongy, flushing spikes. I see vasefuls of calla lilies, armfuls of peonies, and basketfuls of daisies. Of course the three dogwoods are thriving; they will turn orange and crimson, season after season: they will berry and the buds will set as autumn ends, year after year, as if to promise, as they slip into winter slumber, *I am coming back*. The True Love could never tell me that. I rest my head on the back of the chair and wonder at the dignity of the wounded oak. The moon glimmers through the branches.

When my children join me in the garden, I see them as smaller than they are. One is chugging soda from a can but I see him holding high his afternoon bottle of warm milk. One is going off to college, and sits in the garden reading a thick volume of history, but I see him sitting on the steps of the elementary school, waiting for the first day to begin, a fearful, excited look on his small, pale face as he balances a backpack larger than he is.

I suppose we feel time in every direction, in a garden, and that is part of the pleasure of succumbing to its enchantments. It is like the spell cast by a good book, or an evocative poem. There are some that are perfect for reading in the garden: I often take T. S. Eliot's *Four Quartets* out to my armchair under the oak, and feel a deep pleasure in the intricacy of his meditations, as I try to unravel their mysteries, but it is in the garden that I *feel* his meaning: "Time present and time past / Are both perhaps present in time future, / And time future contained in time past." I want to slow time down, for the children, for my own body, for losing love. "Other echoes / Inhabit the garden. Shall we follow?" I want to speed time up, so that I will be around to see the new trees grown thick and tall, the new plants needing division. Sometimes I feel I am in a wonderland of my own making, able to shrink and grow at will, in relation to the way I see my trees and flowers. "Go, said the bird, for the leaves were full of children, / Hidden excitedly, containing laughter." I walk over the path, at a snail's pace, every morning and every evening, coffee cup or wineglass in hand; the path must be taken very slowly, to last long enough to see things a different way.

"Go, go, go, said the bird: human kind / Cannot bear very much reality." I pause every few stepping-stones; where the ground falls off a tiny bit from the stone ledge, I see a valley down below. Where the Buddha sits in meditation under the hemlock, I see an entire room in which I could join him for a nap. Where my armchairs sit, I see the throne of a queen reigning over a land of peace and prosperity. When I was a little girl, I spent hours playing house. Now I am playing garden. I am so tiny that the pitch is steep; I am so gigantic that the shrubs are the tops of trees. Where the path winds through a few trees, I am lost in the woods. And I am waiting, like a lost princess, for the kiss of the True Love to wake me from my long slumber.

Was the garden too good to be true? Did I dream it up? Of course. But in a garden dreams come true. When I see what isn't there, but could be there (and, I'm determined, will one day be there), I'm celebrating the transforming power of love. A garden is the place for an open heart. If you pay enough attention to what is before you, you can see the seeds of what will be. Sure, a rose is always a rose is a rose. When was it not? But like anything alive, it unfolds, it has mystery, it is unpredictable, something that will show you more of what it is in good time. Fantasy, desire, imagination—those are the things that help you stick around for more blooming. Something does, after all, come of all our little labors—not some heavenly reward, but a gift of the gods springing from the very ground on which we stand. It is all around us.

When I have spent a long day weeding through the ground cover—so long that I could weed blindfolded, so familiar is the feel of each plant as I pull it from the ground, the rampant weeds coming easily, deceptively, leaving enough root behind to get started again the moment you leave, the thick, rubbery white roots of the pachysandra resistant, the vinca clinging tenaciously, by a thread, even though it runs shallow—I become a brooding old crone, and I fear for the years ahead, with my back off its hinges, hamstrings pulled too taut, knees scabbarded in pain, the bones in my neck making malicious grinding sounds. Even now, when I am in between youth and old age, I cannot dig the big holes by myself. What will I do years from now? How will I take care of my garden?

But it is to take care of such thoughts that hope was invented. I think, if I am diligent now, by then this garden will shade out its weeds. I will be in no hurry. I will need to rest in every chair, on every bench, at the edge of every stone, along the way. More little ones will have been born of my own little ones, and they, too, will find me on the paths. The days will be short, the years long, just as they were when I was a child. The stroll through the woods will truly be slow and winding—and suddenly I understand that I am planning to be in that garden a long, long time. If I am so lucky.

# FIFTEEN

# FOUNTAIN OF TEARS

*"Love is so short, forgetting is so long."*
—Pablo Neruda
"Tonight I Can Write"

The Boys and I climbed out of the car, finally home, after too long a drive on a congested thruway. We were exhausted. The sun was going down. The golden, evening light of an early spring afternoon was beautiful in the garden, slanting through the sassafras, whose fat mittens of leaves rustled with the faintest breeze and made thousands of shadows dance across the house. I stood on the porch a moment, taking in the burnt glow of the sunset through the trees, and then noticed something unfamiliar at my feet. A small cement statue, no more than six inches tall, of a little boy had been tucked next to the door, his face crumpled up at me with the tiniest pucker of a smile, his tousled, ringletted head arched back, his arms wrapped around knees held close to his chest. A little bunch of a boy. The statue had not been there when we had left, I had never seen it before, and yet the boy looked somewhat familiar. He looked, in the vaguest possible way, like Theo. I liked the impish, cheerful way in which he was waiting for me to come home.

On the other side of the door was another little statue, this one of a woman; her arms were also wrapped around her knees, but her head was buried in her arms. Her long hair was pinned up in a knot at the back of her neck. The little mother, I supposed, wrapped in her dreams. The things were awfully cute, not what I would have bought for myself (only because I try to practice restraint), but I was charmed. The Boys came back outside to get their things from the car, and they noticed the little statues.

"Who are they from, Mom?" Theo asked.

I shrugged my shoulders, and told him I had no idea.

"A secret admirer!" Theo was thrilled. He had learned about secret admirers from Nana, his aunt from New Orleans; they are a very important, and common, part of life in the South.

My secret admirer. Well, I suppose love grows by surprise. As long as I had known him, the True Love had been leaving little gifts around my garden, stacks of wood, pieces of furniture, invasive plants. This was usually the way he would let me know that he was coming back into view. Or that he was on his way out. That's the thing about a garden, he might have said. It's like baseball. Anything can happen at any moment.

There is nothing better than finding gifts in the garden. How could I ever forget being led by my father out into a crisp

October twilight as a seven-year-old, hands over my eyes, as instructed, leaves crinkling underfoot, the cool air against my cheeks—and there it was, leaning against a tree, the turquoise bicycle I had been longing to get for my birthday. Or the gifts from Balthazar, the white-haired, pink-eyed cat with opposable thumbs, polydactyl, I've been told, who, abandoned as a tiny kitten, had crawled into the closet of my college dormitory room and nested in a shoe. I had found him mewling and sucking on a wool sweater that had fallen to the floor and lay bunched at the back of the closet. He grew strong and large in my care, and went home with me to my parents' house for the summer when the term ended. Balthazar was a great killer of birds, but this did not upset me. I love birds, but he was a cat, and it was in his nature to hunt. Balthazar would frequently disappear into the garden at dusk—I could barely follow his ghostly form, catching the last light of the day, as he headed into the woods. I was deeply pleased by his sacrificial offerings, the tender, artful arrangements of wings and flowers he would leave in the garden under my window for me to find in the morning after a long night of hunting. White cats may be magical, but they are also often deaf, I learned too late, when Balthazar did not return one morning, and after days of tearful searching, my mother and I found his body bobbing on a nearby pond, bloated, matted, and stinking. He had been hit by a car; someone had tossed him into the water.

I like making gifts to my garden as well, and that's how I think of all the little things that I put into it—so many things that the place was in danger of looking like a garden store, said the True Love, rather haughtily, I thought, as he was responsible for quite a bit of the stuff. Well, I have an expansive view of what is tasteful. It includes things that give pleasure no matter what they look like. Wind chimes hang deep within the trees and shrubs at each end of the house; some I hear from the kitchen in the morning, some I hear as I drop off to sleep. It thrills me that you can get chimes tuned to so many pitches, nowadays; my favorite one, since I'm a gamelan girl from way back, is the chime based on the notes of that Javanese orchestra's scale. It hangs outside my bedroom door so that I can dream I am playing in a *wayang* again. There are gaily painted Chinese porcelain garden seats strategically placed along the path, should a visitor tire of wending her way through the woods and around the daylilies. There is an old wellhead, from Venice, set now in a bed toward the back, where the sandbox used to be; it was given to me by my beloved mother-in-law, who had been the kind of person who shopped the world on her travels and knew how to ship large, heavy, fragile, and unwieldy treasures back to the States. (I am so inept at this sort of thing that it took me fifteen years to understand that it was possible to place the wellhead deeper into the garden, where it could be admired, rather than keep it at the side of the driveway where the furious movers had rolled it down the ramp off their truck and left it. Leonard, of course, knew exactly how to take care of it.)

The catnip that made the neighborhood cats giddy with pleasure each afternoon had been left by the gift-bearing True Love; naturally it was invasive. Whenever the cats visited, which was frequently, the birds of the garden dived and shrieked and made a ruckus, protecting their nests. I put mint into the garden, for the mint tea my mother had taught me to make—the mint was a gift from my parents' garden, and, of course, it, too, was invasive. The only thing that was stronger was the giant hosta, whose enormous paddles of leaves eventually shaded out most of the mint.

But what a wonderful smell, mint in the middle of a hot day, mingling with the heavy fragrance of rosemary and lavender planted nearby.

When I raked the soggy, matted leaves out of the beds at the end of winter, I would find old metal nameplates, like tiny gravestones, bearing names of plants I had never seen, or long forgotten. When I was digging in beds near the house, the earth would yield up worms wriggling through shards of glass or crockery, mementos of meals and accidents in years past. After the roofers left off their shingling and patching, the ground around the house was littered with coils of copper and bright shreds of foil and scraps of plastic and splinters of cedar. I meant to rake the debris up before winter came, and didn't get around to it. But the birds did, and the next summer, as I was pruning back the clematis that had made a dense cover on the back wall of the house, I was delighted by the discovery of two birds' nests, sparkling with blue foil, the coils of copper woven with straw, the splinters pinching the bottoms tight, plastic banners hanging off the sides. The birds must have thought that I had left all that stuff as gifts for them, for their housekeeping. One of the birds, a catbird, became very friendly that spring (catbirds being sociable creatures). I fed it slices of orange, and it would perch on the tip of my shoe, chattering amiably, while I stretched out on a chaise to read a book. There is an easy society in the garden.

The True Love was a gardener himself, which was perhaps why he understood the charm of gifts left outdoors. In other words, he liked to plant things, and he liked to tend to them, to fuss over them, and he liked all the small ways we have of filling our gardens, bit by bit—which is my definition of a gardener. Someone who puts his hands in the earth (rather than someone who causes everything to be done for him. Not that

ad sort of fellow; I would say he is simply an appre-
gardens, in the Toad tradition).

watching the True Love in his own garden; there
was something sweet and tender about the things he planted.
He moved in the tiniest increments, across his vast grounds, so
that whatever he put into the landscape was swallowed up and
nearly disappeared. He persevered. For unfathomable reasons,
there was something poignant and brave about the sight of
him, alone outside, pushing across a meadow his large wheel-
barrow containing a single lilac bush (that was sure to be
lonely wherever it landed) and vast quantities of manure
(this was a man who believed in manure, and heaped it lavishly around his rosebushes, which had the weird effect of
making circles of grass grow three times taller there than
the rest of the lawn, as if the fairies had been dancing round
the roses all night, and left their telltale fairy rings. (By the way,
I had found *The Little White Bird* to be full of fascinating garden information of this sort. Did you know that flowers are
simply a fairy's daytime disguise? And that if you pay close
attention, you can catch them at transplanting themselves,
which finally explains, and perhaps excuses, the disarray
many of us suddenly confront in our beds.)

One day the True Love had offered to help me get control
of the wisteria growing over my bedroom balcony. It had
become so aggressive that it was threatening to choke the
life out of a nearby yew tree, and pull down the arbor over the
balcony. Its branches had become so thick and tough that I did
not have the strength to close the blades of my pruner around
them.

I must admit the wisteria had proven to be one of my bigger gardening miscalculations. The vine had begun to drill its
way out of the ground one spring years earlier—this was

when I was still married—next to the terrace. It surprised me; I hadn't known anything was under the ground there, and then it astounded me by its reckless determination. In my naivete, I encouraged it, little knowing that I was nurturing a monster—giving it a piece of string to climb to the second story, and going so far as to build an arbor over the balcony for it to climb. I had always thought of wisteria as a Southern plant—mainly because I had not been paying attention to the abundant evidence of its presence in my own neighborhood, hanging from trees and pulling down gutters. I associated it with the sort of grand old ladies with powdery-white skin who were given to fainting spells and vapors; I assumed, because of the delicacy of the blossom, that the wisteria was a swooner as well, and I was thrilled to coax it along in my garden. I was fascinated by its twining habits, and I seemed to have two kinds, one that twined from left to right (clockwise), which I later learned was the Japanese wisteria *(W. floribunda),* and another, climbing up the opposite column of the porch, twining right to left, *W. sinensis,* Chinese wisteria. Though there is an American variety, *W. frutescens,* the wisteria we know best was brought from Asia to the U.S. in the early 1800s, and is now well established here. It is fascinating how our Northeastern gardens are essentially Asian in origin—peonies, rhododendron, azalea, to name a few. Wisteria is too happy a transplant. Now that I am wiser about wisteria, I have seen infestations of it—gleeful escapees from someone's garden—tangled in trees around the neighborhood, some vines having grown as high as sixty or seventy feet; the wisteria will eventually strangle the life out of the tree. I bumped into the former owner of my house at the supermarket one day, and she told me that she and her sister had hacked the wisteria out of her garden ten years earlier; it had pulled down the balustrade and the arbor that had once stood over *her* bedroom balcony. She was shocked to hear that the plant had resurrected itself.

I had the temerity to think I could contain its rampant will. The first mistake I made with it, I now know, was to encourage the growth of the entire vine, rather than to be ruthlessly selective in creating a strong framework of primary branches—that would have been easier to manage. Wisteria must be treated like the most wayward of children—the sort of naughty thing that needs a goblin's spell to bring it into line. Wisteria can grow ten feet a year, and mine did, in every direction. It insinuated itself into the window sashes, sent tendrils corkscrewing between the wood shingles of the house, ripping them off, climbed up the chimney—and would have come down the chimney, too, had I not been forced up on the roof with the pruning shears. It wound its way through the arms and back of the chaise on the porch, found its way into the tubes of the chime, out the other end, and around the clapper, where it proved to be stronger even than the wind. The chime was silenced. I had the feeling that if I sat outside, engrossed in a book long enough, I would soon find myself pinned to my chair by the wisteria. That it would creep into my bedroom while I slept, strangling me.

I could actually *see* the wisteria grow, dementedly throwing off sticky tendrils that would get longer and longer, defying gravity, until they could clamp themselves onto something; only when a tendril was safely anchored would it unfurl its leaves. It seemed to have eyes, or some sort of hidden vision, to know in which direction to hurl itself for support. It curled into the yew near the porch, squeezed the wooden railings until they cracked, rotted constantly, shedding sticks and leaves all summer, and refused, perversely, to yield a single fragrant bloom in the spring, which, as far as I am concerned, is the wisteria's saving grace. Little wonder the old Japanese painters were so devoted to wisteria, with its forceful beauty. There is nothing more heady, in the early spring, than those pendulous racemes of blue or violet or white, hundreds of them drooping and fluttering from a single gnarled old branch that has wound its elaborately polite way through the slats of a pergola, sending a thick, grapelike fragrance out to waft in through the window on a breeze. That is a well-trained plant. But there was no floribunda in mine, and no politesse, either. I had planned to be sitting at my piano in the living room when that fragrant evening breeze rippled through. No such luck. I learned too late that wisteria doesn't bloom well in shade—and the Japanese wisteria does not start blooming until it is ten years old. By which time my house will have been reduced to a rubble of bricks and shingles.

Oddly enough, the wisteria had surfaced at the same time as did the troubles between me and my husband, and from then on I could not help thinking about the unraveling of our marriage in terms of the wisteria: the roots of our problems had been there from the beginning, chopped down to the ground and nicely buried, but as anyone knows who has ever tried to contain the depredations of wisteria, or grapevine, or bittersweet, or wild rose, or Virginia creeper, or honeysuckle, or any one of those vines that choke the life out of that to which they cling so tenaciously, and look beautiful doing it, you have to pull up the deepest part of the root if you want to keep trouble from returning. We had not.

My husband had never gardened with me. It was not something he enjoyed; he did not even like to sit and read in the garden while I worked. It's funny how some people just don't respond to that call, in the same way that some people just aren't interested in cooking, or reading, or swimming. He grew to resent the time I spent in the garden, feeling that I went there to escape the family. I went there to anchor my family life, in the beginning, to send down roots around our house. But, as these things have a way of doing, what he said eventually became true. The garden became my retreat.

So I was delighted by the True Love, who enjoyed digging holes for iris and lilac, and sawing errant limbs off apple trees, and hacking away at vines. He arrived one day, marched right up to the balcony, climbed a ladder, extended the barrel of the clipper as far as it would go, and got to work. I didn't even have to beg. I took the low road with my clippers, and within an hour, there was an impressive tangle of branches at our feet. The yew had been sprung, the railings released, the shingles let go. This, I thought, is like the fairy tales in which the prince hacks his way through the vines to find the princess, kisses her, and brings her back to life, a life of happily ever after, and etc.

Alas, it was not to be; he was an errant prince. Some people want wisteria love, rampant and tenacious. I would have found that smothering. But what I had was hardly better: some sort of maverick perennial, someone who seeded my life with joy, but lived in his own eccentric seasons, and went dormant in the most unpredictable manner. I could never count on his return. Through the Winter of Last Daydreams, stress turned to strain. By spring, it was becoming clear that all that would be left was to deadhead.

Yet I got a taste of the delicious pleasure of gardening in affectionate company. I always thought gardeners fell into two camps about this: there are some who think it is truly enjoyed as the most solitary of pursuits, and some who think it is only bearable with company. But then I understood that there is a way to be deeply together and alone at the same time in a garden, a sort of double solitude—that that is one of gardening's essential pleasures. Couples are always telling me stories about fighting with one another about what the style of the garden ought to be, what should be planted where, what colors are acceptable, what flowers to use, kempt or unkempt, natural or tailored. I have even heard of people stealing out under the cover of night to dig up a hateful flower, or relocate something bothering them. I suppose it is the outdoor equivalent of arguing about paint finishes or sofa styles or, worse, the placement of beds. Trouble in paradise, but still worth a go.

There is nothing to make you wistful like the reminders of pleasures past—the little offerings of love that hang on walls and sit on shelves and tables—and the traces of chores undertaken together. There is nothing to erase all traces of the pleasures of pruning together like wisteria. Within months it was clamoring back into its troublesome ways, as if the True Love had never touched it.

But the gifts left in a garden have an altogether different feel than the ones left in a house, which are often difficult to live with in the absence of love. Those are the gifts that make time stand still. They should usually be put away, at least for a while—paintings stored, teacups wrapped, books shelved, bracelets locked up, boxes of letters sealed—if you want to move on. The gifts in a garden move on themselves to a different life. Somehow, they didn't make me sad, and, like the garden itself, they accrued their own history with every day that passed. I hid the tiny statue of the mother, head in arms, among some pots of red geraniums, and strands of ivy trailed over her knees, so that she could be lost in her own little forest. I tucked her little boy under a tree, to greet me by the door, but only if I thought to look for him. The rain washed over the tiny statutes, the squirrels kicked dirt onto their heads while burying acorns in the potted plants. The summer humidity laid down a moldy coat on the stone table, the catnip got chewed and matted by the doped-up cats. The garden gifts became part of my going on, changing as I did.

The garden continued to yield up its own gifts, and each offering became an odd way of marking the passage of time since the True Love had faded away. He missed the lapis sea of scilla that washed over the feet of the pieris. Their chains of pearly buds seemed to be rising up out of a tidal pool. He missed the bruised glaze laid down on the cold winter earth by the grape hyacinth; he missed feeling the soft carpets of snowdrop underfoot. Those late-winter cousins, galanthus and muscari. Mine had nearly a century of multiplying and dividing behind them, and they were among the first surprises the garden gave me, early that winter, when I was despairing of spring. The snowdrops! In the olden days gypsies would gather them into little bunches supported by an ivy leaf and sell them by the roadside. The True Love missed the daffodils, clutches of them, popping up through the woods, around the base of the porch's columns. He missed the thrilling bells of the malodorous *Fritillaria pallidiflora*. He missed the moonlit clouds of white dogwood, and the ropes of white clematis strung through the "New Dawn" roses; the roses, hundreds of them, a soft pink waterfall cascading down the back of the house; the ripe, narcotic night blooms of the potted datura. Never had the roses been so abundant; never had the clematis made such a fretwork. He missed the rainy voices of the young sassafras. And he missed the blowsy, faintly hysterical staggering of the peonies; then the full-throated chorus line of daylilies. The fine, feathery plumes of the

astilbe announced their arrival. The blossoms of the foxgloves dropped plumply to the ground, empty. The joe-pye
weed tipped top-heavily. The coneflower sprawled across
the bed. The phlox, wreathed in the perfume of an older
generation, turned pale and powdery. The windflower
anemone showered the bed with its elegant white petals
through August and September. By the time the hosta was
lofting its giant, perfumed wands, and the hydrangea was
bursting forth with its bouquet of green-white buds, I realized the True Love had missed the whole thing. And that
every day I had missed him, and I had thought, what a
shame, not to have shared this perfect day; there will never
be another day as extravagantly beautiful.

But the garden had transmitted its pleasures to me.

One day at the end of the summer, while I was away from
home (as was his wont), the errant prince, to whom I was no
longer speaking at all, delivered a surprise for my garden
that enraged me. A gift so heavy that it could not be budged,
I found, when I nearly broke my toe kicking it.

It was a fountain.

That spring, I had almost given myself the fountain I had
always wanted. When Leonard talked me out of it, I thought
ruefully how the fountain had always slipped out of my
grasp. There had always been a good reason, over the years—
a fountain cost too much, it was too much trouble, we were
moving, where would it go, what would it look like, what
would we do with it, and etc. My husband had been against
fountains. I had said as much, one day, to the errant prince in
a fit of pique on hearing from my son that his father and the
new wife were building a new garden—(he was *gardening*?)—
at their new house. Their new garden was full of stone walls.
And a fountain. It wasn't enough that they had just had a new

baby. They had to have a new fountain, too. It set me off. What can I say? Except that the seeds of jealousy were first planted in a garden.

Don't worry, *I* will get you a fountain someday, said the True Love, nobly, boldly, bigheartedly. He did deliver—upon absenting himself.

Worse yet was that the fountain, made of hundreds of pounds of concrete, had to be plugged in. I refused to make a single effort toward accepting it. When, after a few days, I calmed down from the rage of finding the fountain in my garden, no prince attached, my curiosity got the better of me. It wasn't the fountain's fault that it made me furious. (After all, hasn't humankind, since the beginning of time, or at least the seventh day, always found its best rationalizations in the garden?) I wondered what it would sound like, a fountain in the garden. It was a sound I had wanted to hear for years. (Sound being by far the most important part of a fountain.) No one was around to witness my breakdown in willpower. I filled the basin with water, and plugged the contraption in.

The worst was yet to come. The fountain sputtered into action. With a harsh, sucking sound it gathered water up its neck, then began to spit it out its mouth, and, to my dismay, went on to dribble and drool obscenely. Water spilled down the front of its neck, its back, its sides, everywhere but back into the basin. Soon I would hear only the sound of a pump grinding and burning itself out. Within minutes the fountain was sitting in its own pool, and I was once again in a puddle of angry tears. This was most definitely not the fountain of my dreams. I opened an envelope I had not noticed before, that had been taped to the back of the fountain, and read the helpful suggestions from the True Love for correcting the leak, such as siliconing a copper plate to the mouth, or tipping the thing forward or backward or sideways to give it better balance.

That did it. Who gives a girl a faulty fountain?

The fountain of tears. Just the sight of the fountain began to inspire a burble of evil thoughts. I had heard that the True Love was moving to London. I read in the papers about 250,000 demonstrators in the streets protesting the banning of foxhunting by hounds. I wondered, hopefully, if the True Love may have been trampled underfoot. Every time I looked at the fountain, unplugged, its short black cord curled idly in its lap, I wanted to scream. It was hideous. Unacceptable. And implacable. There it sat.

Of course I did not want the prince to retrieve it. (And, as it turned out, he could not have picked it up; he had only gotten it into my garden by driving around town until he found some beefy-enough-looking strangers on the sidewalk, and asked them to come to my house with him and help him move it out of his car, but that's the sort of nutty thing he would do that I found so endearing.) So I called Leonard, the Most Helpful Man.

Leonard looked at the thing dubiously. "Yup," he said. "I sell those. Nice-looking." He stopped, diplomatically.

"But Leonard," I said, "they don't work. They are not properly designed. They leak. You know that. You actually sell these things?"

"You have to get it absolutely level," he said. "Totally level. With a level. And then you can silicone the—"

"No. I will not silicone the mouth. There is no such thing as level in a garden. It was a gift. It makes me cry. It makes me furious."

"Oh. One of *those* things," Leonard said. "Well, I don't want to pry—"

"Never mind. You don't need to know."

Leonard's face lit up.

"Oh! Well, then. Do you want me to get the sledge-hammer?" he said, rather too gleefully. "Smash it up for you?"

Sadly, I am not a violent person.

"We have to move it. Well, *you* have to move it."

By then Leonard knew me well enough not to make further helpful suggestions. He came over later that week with some of his men, and they put the thing in my garage. I draped a heavy, quilted, turquoise blue mover's cloth over it to ward off the evil eye. And there it sits.

The fountain of tears.

# SIXTEEN

# WHY PRUNE?

*"don't tell us
how to behave in
anger, in longing, in loss, in home-
sickness, don't tell us,
dear friends."*
—Mary Oliver
"On Losing a House"

"The following is the result of the math in accordance with the literature concerning the structural condition of your pin oak," the fax began. "We will reduce its size and its resistance to the wind accordingly. Trunk diameter = 31.8 inches which = 804 inches square. Decay column = 24 inches = 452 inches square. 452 divided by 804 = 56%. The 4-inch cavity opening = 4% of the 100-inch circumference. The total decayed area is 60% therefore the total structural loss is 40%. Given the fact that pin oak is very strong wood, I believe that this number is very conservative."

Mr. D'Ambrosio had returned with a fax. I felt sick. The fate of my tree seemed to be hanging in a cat's cradle of calculations; I could make no sense of it. Mr. D'Ambrosio suggested we make an appointment to talk about it face-to-face. "I know how much that tree means to you," he said kindly. *"Ciao, ciao."* As he had taken to saying every time he hung up the phone. He was so jaunty.

Mr. D'Ambrosio arrived early a few mornings later. I watched him, glumly, from my bedroom window as he parked his car, got out, smoked a quick cigarette, and stood awhile looking up at the trees.

"What a place. What a beautiful place," he said. I thought, What a lovely way to greet a garden. I remarked that he looked tanned and healthy. "I've been fishing," he said. "Over to Montauk. In a boat. Deep-sea fishing. It is gorgeous out there. I catch blues, striped bass, whatever's running. I try to fish every weekend of the summer."

I wondered if he could give Leonard a few pointers on escaping from his overtaxed life; but then again, the men were at opposite ends of their careers. Mr. D'Ambrosio had been caring for sick trees for several decades, and could probably afford the time for fishing. My theory was confirmed, of course, when I got my first bill from him. But some things I will pay for happily, and the care of my trees is at the top of the list. We strolled, very slowly, over to the oak at the far side of the yard. I was dragging my feet. I didn't want to hear about the surgery.

"That maple," Bob began, startling me out of my gloom. He

was pointing into the neighbor's yard. "What a mess. Healthy, but a mess. Badly pruned; someone took out a limb off the side that has made the balance of the tree shift radically."

I explained that most of that limb had fallen down, and I suddenly realized that, had my children been a few years younger when the limb had fallen, it would have crashed on their swing set, which was no longer standing. That tree just did not like having children under it.

"I'm going to get in there, next spring, and clean that thing out. The canopy needs opening up; a couple of those big, low branches should come off. Maybe that tree will straighten itself out, over time. I won't do anything until spring. That tree shouldn't be pruned heavily before winter. Don't worry. I understand what an eyesore that back is. By the way, I notice some of the bittersweet is dead. Did they cut it?"

I explained that I had pulled out what was coming out of the wall, and I confessed that I had reached into the privet and cut the vines that were clambering into the dogwood. I was afraid to reach too far into the mess, for fear of disturbing the now-calm relations.

"Good. But I have to get it by the roots. I'm planning to do that. We have to get this cleaned up. And when I prune that maple, you'll get more light in here."

Well, Bob certainly had a way of delivering the good news first. Then came the bad.

"The oak is rotted. We have to cut away forty percent of the branch growth. That's what I was trying to show you by my calculations. I'm not going to do that this fall; it would be too severe. I don't know what kind of winter we are going to have. But I am going to have my men climb up there and take away a lot of the vertical growth, some branches and all the suckers. That way the wind will go through the branches, instead of pushing against them, as I explained earlier. Is that okay?"

That much was fine. What terrified me was losing forty percent of the branch growth. I looked up at the tree, and tried to imagine half of it gone.

"What we do is, we cut the branches back so they don't extend so far."

"You mean, you just lop them off? Midway?" This went against everything I had ever heard about proper pruning. But really, what did I know, compared with someone who had made it his life's work? "Just lop off the branches?"

"Yes. No—"

"But that sounds brutal. How is that going to look?"

"Terrible," Bob said. "That's called pollarding. But that's not what I'm going to do to your oak. That's what I need to do on that Norway maple. Bring it in, in a good way, make the tree smaller. Your oak has been lion-tailed. So has that maple, by the way. You know how lions' tails look, at the circus? That means stripping all the branches off a limb until you get to the end. That makes these long, rangy branches. That is *not* what we are going to do. That's what a lot of other people do. That is wrong. We are going to do some very selective pruning, cut back to secondary branches, so the limb will continue to grow. Listen, I know how you feel about that tree. I can see that you are a very sensitive person. Very sensitive. I am going to be very delicate in this operation. You won't even notice I've done anything. Very, very delicate."

I told him I felt terrible about the whole thing, which he knew. That I felt as if I had been neglectful in my caretaking of the tree.

"Listen, that decay has been going on fifty years at least. No one told you. You've had guys up there, pruning. That's clear.

You couldn't see that hole from down here. You saw how high it was. You could only see it from up in the tree—or from uphill. I take it you haven't spent a lot of time in your neighbors' house. The guys pruning, they should have told you. But most people don't know. They don't know what they're looking at. They look at things, and they don't see trouble right in front of them. They don't see it."

There was nothing to say about that. I knew he was right.

"I'll tell you what I'm going to do," Mr. D'Ambrosio said. He began steering me away from the oak, toward the stand of sassafras in front. "I'm going to take you on a drive upstate, not far from here, and I am going to show you a garden that you will adore. You will fall in love with it. I promise you. I put it in for a friend of mine, he wanted it for his wife; she was always running around, couldn't sit still, relax. It is a woodland garden. It has paths running through the trees, and I planted hundreds of wildflowers in it. All different kinds; we ordered them from small specialty nurseries all over the country. I made her a big chart on my computer—Excel, you know?— with all the names of the plants, and their location along the path, and a description of them, their color, their size, and when they bloom. We planned it so something is blooming all the time. And you just look it up on the computer, to identify it. The wife loves it. She sits around all the time in it. It is so beautiful."

I noticed that whenever Mr. D'Ambrosio hit me with bad news, he replenished me with tiny, wonderful gifts. Bloodroots. Woodland plants. He was always taking my eye back to ground level, which was an odd technique for a guy who kept his eye trained on the branches most of the time.

"You could do a path in these woods, through the sassafras. You aren't taking advantage of them. You don't really have a way into them. And you could plant so much more in here, wild orchids, all kinds of beautiful things, under the trees. You could put a contemplation bench in here."

I could see it already, and it was perfect; I could see where the path would begin, how the first stepping-stones would be set, how you would have to be in the side garden in order to find your way into the front walk, which azaleas it would wend its way through, where the bench could be, what would need to be planted around the little bench to give the bench a screen from the street—and would the bench be wood? Did I have enough wood in the garden already? A little stone bench? Old?—

"We'll give the sassafras a good pruning next week, let in a little more air and light here. That sassafras, by the way, is rotting from a drainpipe that has collapsed. The water isn't getting all the way to the drains. It's flooding the trees. You'll have to call your roofer. Put a new leader on the gutter, leave it out of the ground. We'll put a big stone slab under the end of the pipe to disperse the water. You like stone? I have some great stone. A beautiful piece of feldspar, all sparkling, gorgeous color. I'll bring it over. You call the roofer. I'll take you to the woodland garden. You'll love it. You'll see what to do next."

By now we were back around in the front garden, peering into the woods, as, with the True Love gone, I felt free to call it. I began to ask him for the names of some of the other trees mixed into the sassafras, to make sure I had them right. Another oak, a younger one, a red oak, coming along beautifully. A couple of wild cherry, whose fruit left dark red stains all over the ground; the birds feasted on the berries. An ash. And then one that stopped Mr. D'Ambrosio. I had mistakenly thought it was another cherry, as their bark is similar.

"That is a black birch," he said. "That is a beautiful tree. How nice that you have one; you don't see them that often, but you should. We should have more of them in our gardens. The black birch is what gave us an economic leg up when we were settlers."

He looked at me to make sure I was paying proper attention, which of course I was.

"Wintergreen comes from black birch. Native Americans made birch beer, boiling the sap and adding honey and fermenting it. Must have been delicious. And the twigs made great toothbrushes. Black birch was used to treat intestinal worms, rheumatism, so many problems."

I was slowly becoming impressed with how many of my trees had medicinal—or beverage—value. To most of us suburban gardeners, trees are simply decorative. I look at them for long hours on end, and appreciate the way they keep the house cool and shaded in summer, and admire the extravagant colors of their foliage in autumn. That is all I do with trees. But here were people eating, and drinking, and staying alive and healthy by their trees.

"But the most important thing about wintergreen," Mr. D'Ambrosio was saying. "When the settlers came to America, syphilis was rampant in Europe. Everyone was dying of it. Doctors thought, at the time, that a wintergreen salve, applied topically, was a cure for syphilis—what a horrible disease; you know anything about it?—so the settlers had a big market. They cut down the trees, boiled them, extracted the oils, and sold it by the barrels in Europe.

"That's why I like that tree. And the leaf, you know, is the leaf on the package of Breyer's ice cream. You know that ice cream? You remember that leaf? That's a black birch.

"That's why I love my work. There are so many stories in

trees. So much history. Of course, trees are crucial to civilization. No one could ever take us over, because of our trees."

At this point he lost me. Stories about ice cream logos and the cure for diseases—even if they turned out to be misinformed or half-truths—were vastly entertaining. But I had never considered the political, or strategic, value of trees. Bob had.

"A country that has trees is a safe country. There are places to hide—"

A man after my own heart.

"—and we have trees, in America. We have plenty of trees. No one could ever take us over. Look at Vietnam. A tiny, little country. But full of trees. Covered with trees. Vietnamese soldiers hid in the trees. The trees protected the people. And we couldn't take that country, tiny as it was.

"But look at Iraq. No trees. Go right in, take it out. Boom. No problem. Defenseless."

It was quite an unusual, and interesting, view of global politics. I had to admit that I certainly felt well defended, behind my suburban trees.

Over the next few days, I thought long and hard about whether to let Mr. D'Ambrosio return with his cutting tools. Part of me really wanted to leave everything alone. Maybe ignore the problem; I had been ignorant up until then. The trees did not really need our help. Why couldn't the wind and the rain do their work, and tear off sodden limbs and topple the dead ones? Why would we interfere, crawling onto branches with saws, branches that had borne the weight of countless gales? I knew the easy answer, of course. Why couldn't I live in a forest, where for every tree that falls, three have already risen to take its place? I thought about deadwood, and about being top-heavy, and about decay. It was better to attack it, get rid of it.

If trees are the giant spirits that surround us, we should tend to them. You can think of gardening—with its weeding and pruning and clearing and planting—as a way to "act with vigor in the face of uncertainty," as Bertrand Russell, in his nineties, described what was necessary in confronting old age. It is satisfying work—you can see the results immediately (although in some cases, like weeding the lawn, you won't see the results the next day because the weeds return overnight). In a suburban garden, we take care of what is not sound in the hope that it doesn't bring everything else down. We saw those limbs off because we have seen what is rotted, weak, infested, attenuated. We prune so as not to have a cascading failure of nerve.

One night I woke from a vivid dream, tears washing my face. They were not miserable tears; they were full of joy. I wrote the dream down, half-conscious, but aware that it was important, and then I fell back to sleep immediately. The next day the dream was forgotten, but I noticed the pad of paper on which I recorded it, and I was startled that the dream was about the oak tree.

There is a huge storm. I go out into the garden afterward to find that all my trees have been knocked down. Someone— a giant, for the dream occurs in a time of giants—has already picked up the fallen trees, leaning them on the fence, at the far corner of the yard, neatly stacked, standing upright, one against the other. Dozens of trees have been ripped up. The oak, my beloved oak, which I recognize immediately, is at the front of the pile.

The top of the oak has broken off. Still, the tree easily reaches sixty feet high. The trunk has been sheared in half, cross-sectioned, sliced open from top to bottom. I can see a large mass of rotted wood at the top, at the break, and I can see the rot as it narrows and tunnels deeper into the tree. The tunnel stops at what appears, improbably, to be a piece of furniture in the tree.

I step closer to make sure my eyes are not deceiving me. There stands, carved into the tree, an enormous armoire. The wood on the front is burled, polished and gleaming. I open the door of the armoire from the bottom edge, which I can barely reach, it is so high off the ground. Something is engraved inside the bottom edge of the door, on a golden label; it says *Browning Oak*. I push the door all the way open. It is massive, very heavy, I have to put my weight against it; its hinges creak. I step back into the garden to look up at the armoire. Inside the armoire are some shelves, and a long space with a rod across the top, for hanging clothes. Everything about this piece of furniture is oversize. Either that, or I have become very tiny. There is already hanging, in the armoire, a blue satin dress, like a ball gown. It has a full skirt, it is gathered at the waist, and has long, transparent sleeves. It is a beautiful, enchanting, thrilling gown, easily the sort of thing a princess would wear. I stare at it.

I stand in front of the tree in awe, wondering how the dress got in there. How could the cupboard door have been opened before the tree was split? I do not wonder how the wardrobe would have been carved in the trunk to begin with. That I take at face value. I call my father to come over and have a look. He loved to build things of wood—he had built the headboard, complete with bookshelf, for my childhood bed; I knew he would like the wardrobe. We wonder about the whole thing together, and we admire it, too. It is a gorgeous piece of furniture, and it seems to have given the tree a new life. I wake, my face washed with glad tears.

Later, during the day after the dream, I remembered where

I had first seen that dress—it was a costume I had worn in a play in junior high school. I think I played the part of a princess—and could the play have been *Camelot?* I cannot remember anything about the experience, which must have been terrifying for me, a shy person. The stage fright, the memorizing of the lines, even whether or not I sang—all forgotten. All I remembered was the blue of that dress, and the satiny material, and also a velvet sash that was tie-dyed (this was the sixties) with dappling blues that went from deep royal shades to the light blue of a sunny sky; I must have been a delphinium of a princess. My mother, in a generous gesture of enthusiasm, had had the dress made for me, and we had chosen the sash together at the fabric store—I remembered that trip—and for years afterward, I fingered the sash rapturously, as it hung in the closet, pinned to the dress, unworn, for how many chances do you have to be a princess?

I did not venture into too much of an analysis of the dream, as I thought about it during the day, mainly because I did not want to. It was so beautiful, on its own, that I did not want to embellish it (or shrink it), beyond understanding that it revealed the intensity of my feelings for the trees, and for the roots of my garden and for my family. The trees gave my tiny country protection and defense. They were born before us, and would live on long after us. Yes, you can tell years' worth of weather—drought, rain, heat—from the condition of each ring. But even more, the trees were magical. They were repositories for so much of what goes on in the garden. There is a reason we speak of family trees. It was time for me to take proper care of the one bequeathed to my garden.

Several weeks later, just as I was beginning to wonder if he had abandoned me, Mr. D'Ambrosio and his team arrived, bearing coils of heavy rope and saws. One man climbed high

up into the oak. Another truck pulled halfway up the driveway, extended two heavy metal pods out to either side, and
stabilized itself. A long extension arm with a bucket on the
end carried another man up into the sassafras. The cutting
began.

Mr. D'Ambrosio took a stroll around the garden with me.
We peered up at the men in the trees. One of them, an extremely
tall and lanky black man, was wearing a high, gaily colored knit
turban.

"Ah, Sly," said Mr. D'Ambrosio. I could feel a story coming
on. "How I found Sly? Up a tree in St. Croix. You know,
weaving is my hobby. Weaving anything. I weave with straw,
banana leaves, yarn, you name it. I love to weave." Mr. D'Ambrosio looked over to see how I was taking this.

"Weaving is my passion. So one day I was weaving in
St. Croix, where I had gone because of the coconut leaves.
You know, I go on vacations to weave. I ran out of supplies,
and Sly there shot up a tree and got more for me. I said to
him, 'Anytime you need some extra money, the way you
climb trees, you come up to New York and work for me.
Anytime.' He arrived a few months later, and there he is, in
your tree."

Leonard arrived unexpectedly. "Hey, Bob, I haven't seen
you around for a while," he said.

"Yeah, well, I thought I had a heart attack," Mr. D'Ambrosio said. "I went to the hospital. It was just heartburn. But
I was scared. I've cleaned up my act. No more drinking. No
more smoking." He patted his neck and showed us his nico-
tine patch.

Leonard patted his arm. "Me, too. Patch. Happens at the
end of every summer. I chew tobacco while I'm fishing, then
I have to quit."

"You catch any sea bass?"

"I'm into whitefish now. Whitefish is the best."

Mr. D'Ambrosio told a joke he had heard from a friend on his boat. Apparently, lots of jolly things happen on fishing boats, I was learning. "So a guy is at a party, and he tells his friends what he got his wife for Christmas last year. A plot in a cemetery. She says to him, Whaddya get me this year? Nothing, he says. You didn't use last year's present." The men guffaw amiably. Mr. D'Ambrosio pointed out the sun coming through the sassafras; the leaves were so thin they were nearly translucent and the light was diffused, as if it were coming through stained glass. We all strolled around to the back of the house.

We looked up at the Norway maple; Leonard asked after its fate.

"We're going to pollard that tree, make it think it's young again."

"Really?" said Leonard. "Does that work for humans?"

"Sure, Leonard. Look at you, with your crew cut. You're pollarding yourself.

"Not the oak, honey," he said, taking in the stricken look on my face. "Delicate surgery. Very delicate. You won't even know I've done a thing." Then Mr. D'Ambrosio turned toward the house. *"Ciao, ciao,"* he said. "But before I go, one more thing. What about that wisteria?" I must have looked unnerved. Bob D'Ambrosio seemed to have a radar for all kinds of trouble.

"Don't get me wrong, wisteria is a wonderful thing. Beautiful. I like that curtain you made there in front of your porch. But do you get any blooms? I thought not. I'm going to take care of this for you. I'm going to bang the bark, beat it up a bit. The plant will think it's in trouble. 'Uh-oh. I gotta reproduce,' it will say to itself. 'I might die, so I have to produce a new generation.' It will send out flowers, berries, seeds. That's what they do with walnuts, you know. They go around with baseball bats and beat on the trees. It gives you a good crop.

"So I'll come out and bruise this thing a bit. You'll see. Next spring you will have so many blossoms. And I have a guy who is great on wisteria. It's almost all he does, vines. He'll thin that whole thing for you, get the top of that untangled. You probably aren't even sitting under it anymore, it is so dense and dank. He'll pick a few leaders, follow them up, prune the top, and keep that green curtain you've got going at the bottom."

Well. Who needs the True Love? Bob D'Ambrosio did not even have to say, Don't worry. Everything will be fine.

I knew it would.

# SEVENTEEN

# TEENAGERS IN THE HOSTA

*"Across her face there seemed to pass many feelings and reflections: it was as if she ached to touch and gather in and make whole those scattered years of change. But how can time be gathered in and kissed? There is only flesh."*

—John McGahern
*By the Lake*

One day, later in the autumn, I was taking my early-morning walk through the new garden, steaming cup of coffee in hand, dew cooling my feet, inspecting the health and measuring the progress of all the new plants we had put in that spring. I love the morning rounds because the traffic is still and the birds are in full song.

Also because I go to bed believing in the powerful magic of the night, believing that when I wake everything that was crooked will be straight, everything that was weak will be strong, everything that languished will be bold. At least in the garden.

That morning I was walking with Leonard, who started his workday as the sun came up. He told me that this garden had become one of his favorite jobs. He was very proud of the work we had done; he felt it had called on his creative powers. Even the pink cords.

"But I'm exhausted," Leonard said. "I can't believe how busy I am. I try to be little, I get big. That azalea doesn't look so good. I might have overfertilized. I don't know. I mean, your soil—well, let's just say we had to do a lot of preparation.

"But that's it. I'm going fishing. I'm going to Alaska. Just me. Not the wife. Not the kids. Just me, the boat, the water. You want any halibut? You want *more* hosta?"

We were trying to finish up the planting, fill in the gaps, rearrange, before his trip; really, it would never end. Toward the back, we noticed a bunch of ferns that yesterday had been thriving, and today were trampled. We bent to inspect this fresh mystery.

"Hmm," said Leonard, putting on his best detective manner, and poking around the crestfallen clumps. "Look at that. All the stems are broken at the same spot."

I felt we were on the trail of some wild, mysterious animal, and I glanced up at the trees nervously, as if it might pounce on us. "What do you think, Leonard? Skunks? Raccoons? Possums? Something bigger?"

Leonard has a flair for the dramatic. He drew himself up, and took a deep breath. "Bigger? I'll say. Teenagers."

We followed the telltale trail of trampled stalks to the

little bench under the oak tree. Leonard went on to tell me that his wife had grown up in this town, and she knew all about the allure of my house. Or more particularly, my garden.

I can see the appeal. As can the teenagers. As they have for several generations, it seems. My house has been lost for years behind the sassafras trees, the azaleas, the rhododendrons. It is true that many a time, as I have crawled under the tent of an azalea eight feet tall to do some pruning, I have found abandoned beer cans. (One surprise involved a six-pack, drained but completely intact, all six cans still secured in their plastic rings, and I sat awhile pondering this accomplishment, wondering who would want to drink beer this way, and why, and who was being impressed by this tribal rite.) From time to time, I have bumped into kids sitting on my boulders under the sassafras trees, puffing langourously away on cigarettes and joints. (And no, I do not call the police, and I hardly need to tell them to stop, so panicked are they by my sudden appearance at the party.)

The front garden is a mecca during Mischief Night, the night before Halloween. The kids throw rolls and rolls of toilet paper into the yard, for the sheer pleasure of watching the thin white tissue blaze through the air and hang in banners off the azaleas. It is a nice effect, really, especially in the moonlight, and also saves me a trip to the grocery store for supplies, as the teenagers' parents seem to stock a good-quality toilet paper.

Once, only once, was there real damage; some obnoxious kids wandered in and heaved a boulder at the little concrete Buddha minding his business on a ledge in the middle of the pool of pachysandra. He had sat there for years, the gift of a friend who was himself an angry man; I wondered if the Buddha had some karmic connection to people's anger. The impact cracked the Buddha's neck but he kept his head. Theo and I discovered this treachery before school one morning. We moved the Buddha around to another part of the garden, and sat him under the hemlock tree. The change would do everyone good. Theo suggested we cover up the patch of lost plaster; it looked so sad. We tied a red kerchief around his neck. (The True Love had wadded the hankie into my hand during a performance of *La Bohème,* as I was responding overheatedly to the drama of hopelessly tragic love. This is the sort of thing a girl folds up, without washing, and tucks into her sock drawer, stuck as she is in a karmic stage of yearning.) (My friend the Nomad, who had spent many years living in an ashram in India, was truly disgusted when I recounted the tale of the broken Buddha. "You've missed the whole point," he said. "You've missed the lesson of the Buddha. You must not form attachments." I ignored him, as there was a little too much detachment going on in my life at the time.)

Theo and I adjusted the folds of the kerchief to cover all the injuries, and the Buddha fell back into the sort of profound repose of which only a Buddha is capable. Theo and I contemplated, with some irritation, the eternal truth of the changeable nature of reality, before calling the police.

The police officer who responded, a beautiful and sympathetic young woman with long, thick red hair, walked through the house with us and into the side of the garden.

"Well," she said after a thorough inspection of the damage. "Teenagers."

She took a look around the rest of the garden. I wondered if she were looking for footprints. "I grew up in this town," she said. "I always wanted to see this house. We all thought it was haunted." True enough. And now so is my garden. By teenagers. So much for the sanctity of a garden in suburbia.

Hey. I was a teenager once upon a time. Weren't you? Still,

it took me a while, after finding the trampled ferns, to get comfortable with the idea of kids taking midnight strolls through the pachysandra—particularly since they were probably doing more than strolling. I mean, it is sort of a pain in the neck to dig holes in the dirt and pour in the money (which is, after all, the bottom line in gardening) and then, because someone else is having fun necking, see your work get stomped.

Then I thought about how much pleasure it had given me, to plant things, and scatter around inviting benches and beautiful urns and tinkling chimes, and then feel time pass and let memory visit. A garden, like a home, is a place where love should flourish; why else would it be filled with rooms and beds? There are all kinds of hauntings in the garden. But suddenly it occurred to me, maybe it was the teenagers who were casting the spells. Maybe they were part of the powerful magic of the night, drawing strength up out of the earth.

Maybe the ultimate magic, in any garden, is the chance to breathe in the fragrance of lilies glowing in moonlight and wrap your arms around someone you love.

# EIGHTEEN

# ONE ENCHANTED EVENING

*"... Weather abroad*
*And weather in the heart alike come on*
*Regardless of prediction."*
—Adrienne Rich
"Storm Warnings"

While the planting of the new garden was under way, I had decided to throw a big party. A deadline was in order. It was the first time (though I am at a ripe age) I had undertaken such a large social event. I tend to enjoy my guests solo, or in bunches of two or four, eight at the outside. But a friend was getting married for the first time (though she, too, was at a ripe age, which made the prospect terrifying) and I felt it important, to counterweight her panic, that we mark the occasion festively and generously. I set a date safely in the future, invited sixty of her closest friends, and went back to work, with greater determination, on the garden. Parties are motivating events. All sorts of things get cleaned up because company is coming.

It may seem odd that the first place I went, in anticipation of entertaining, was the garden. But I had decided that hers was to be a garden party; it had to be, my house being too small to contain sixty people, no matter how close they were. And I liked the sound of it, a garden party. Never mind that I had no intention of pitching tents in the event of bad weather; we were in the midst of a severe drought, one that had been unrelenting all summer, and protection from rain would have been impossible, as my garden had no squares or rectangles to speak of in which to set up a tent. In short, I was perfectly ill-prepared for the challenge, but luckily, I was just as happily naive. So a garden party it was to be.

The only part of the garden that wasn't going to be ready was the New Back Bed, the one I had started with, in front of the new wall. In the course of creating the new side garden I realized the Back Bed was all wrong. I had gone so far as to take all the shade plants I had put in the previous spring out of that brilliantly sunny bed and tuck them under the dogwoods and hemlock. The New Back Bed was to become a real flower bed, but what was planted at that point was so immature and straggly that the bed was really a strip of mulch. A gardening friend—a city gardener, so he knew about empty terraces—suggested I bank potted plants in front of the young bed. As he was being forced to leave his apartment, with its terrace garden, I inherited dozens of his potted plants, filled with peonies, fountain grasses, papaver, coleus, roses, dahlias, geraniums. They were all different sizes, so he grouped them in clusters around the new bed, tall ones at the back, and mixed the colors in a satisfying way. Potted plants are a terrific fix, and not only in a pinch, to hide problems. I have known gardeners who take tender tropicals outdoors for the summer, and spot them, for their vivid colors and textures, here and there in perennial beds or pools of shade.

By late summer we were in the midst of a drought of the sort that had become an official state of emergency. It didn't rain anymore. We were also in the middle of an unprecedented heat wave. The day of the party, the thermometer registered 102 degrees by three in the afternoon. I have no air-conditioning. The drought had been going on for such a long time that reservoirs were drying up, the watering of gardens was severely curtailed, and ice water at the table in a restaurant was provided only upon request. The sprinkler system I had had installed was the most efficient way to conserve water, and the watering of gardens, even if very limited, was critical, for it helped no one, in the long run, if trees and plants withered and died. Things were green, in my yard, but not luscious.

On the afternoon of the party, the sky was mysteriously clouding up. Well, perhaps that would cut the heat. My friends and I rolled several small round tables into the garden, and set them up on what remained of the grass. We unwrapped dozens of fat candles, and unpacked dozens of hurricane lamps, bought in deeply discounted bulk, a bargain too good to pass up. (You can never have too many hurricane lamps to protect the candles in the garden—and candles are the only appropriate way to light a garden at night.) The caterer arrived, with a dozen men and women to help serve. Having decided that my kitchen was much too small to prepare food for sixty, we had agreed that she would bring only food that needed warming.

The chef marched her troops into the kitchen, began unpacking dozens of mysterious boxes, and put three men sitting on the sofa to work shelling peas. Within half an hour, a truck rolled up the driveway and proceeded to dump, in front of the garage, a barbecue grill the size of a Ping-Pong table. Seven bags of charcoal and boxes of matches later, the chef had a fire roaring.

Then came the rains.

I had not seen such a torrential downpour since the day a year earlier that the wall had fallen down. Cooks, waiters, friends, and family, all stood at the kitchen window, watching in despair that turned to horror as it began to hail, and large ice cubes began to bounce off the tables and collect in the potted plants. I went up to my bedroom, and there my friend Lora found me an hour later.

"What are you doing?" she said.

"I am staring stupidly out the window," I replied, sitting cross-legged on my bed. "There is nothing I can do. We're finished."

"No-o-o-o-o. This is a great development," she said. "It is only five in the afternoon. The party starts at seven. This way the rain will be over by dinner."

I looked at her, stunned. Where does such cheer come from?

The rain began to let up after half an hour, and we came back to life a bit, riffling stacks of napkins, putting candles into the glass columns, and then the skies yellowed and darkened and opened up and poured down their wrath again; this happened three times, and each time I grew gloomier and Lora grew brighter.

As the third storm eased into a gentle drizzle, and we began to sweep ankle-deep puddles off the porches and terraces, Lora asked me about lighting the candles. What was I waiting for? I must have looked at her as if she had lost her mind, but she said, "In India, they light the candles in the rain all the time."

India. Why not? We seemed to have developed a monsoon season.

We took umbrellas out into the drizzle, and started placing the glass lamps, and their golden beeswax pillars, along the curves of the beds, under trees, by the sides of paths, on rocks, and on tables. I began to light the candles. The sky was ominously darkening yet again, but this time it turned out to be evening coming on. One by one the damp candles spluttered and flickered and then the wicks dried and caught and flared up tall, and gradually, as the drizzle let up, the garden began to glow in the soft light.

The foliage was heavy with water, branches hanging in graceful arcs, gently, sweetly dripping, the green of the leaves as profound a color as I have ever seen. As the temperature dropped into the balmy eighties, a mist began to rise up off the ground and hang in the air. The plants seemed to have thickened in the soaking. Tiny, lacy spider's hammocks beaded with rain glistened in the grass. The garden had never been so enchanting. The fireflies came out, and began to blink and twinkle through the trees. (Fireflies must have been the inspiration for Tinkerbell, with her lamp that turned on and off.) Lora and I moved the porch sofa to the edge of the lawn and set the coffee table in front of it to clear space on the porch for a bar. We lit a few more lamps, and then sat quietly for a few minutes, breathing in the magic of the garden.

"See?" said Lora. "You should always light the candles."

Sixty people arrived; some kicked off their fancy heels and

gamely tiptoed through puddles. Only one person slipped and sprained a wrist; his name was Romeo and he was serving whiskey sours. It seemed like one casualty was pretty good for a garden party, which for some reason I had always imagined to be intensely fraught, raucous affairs. The waiters were so efficient at whisking away glasses as soon as they were put down that guests were constantly returning to the bar; soon everyone had lost track of how much they had drunk. The cook presented one of the most delicious meals I had ever eaten, grilled on the vast contraption that was now merrily blazing under the only tent we had managed to set up. The bride-to-be, and her intended, were beaming. Amazingly (to me, anyway, as my head was still full of little white birds and Peter Pan), the groom's family name was Darling.

To my surprise, my older son showed up for dinner. I had invited him, but Alex had shrugged me off, cagily saying nothing, the way teenagers do when they want to leave open their options. He was wearing a white shirt and shorts, and he looked handsome and poised. I watched him arrive from across the garden; he found my sister and several of the friends he had known through his childhood, and took a seat at a table with them. Their conversation looked animated. I could not bring myself to go over and greet him. I wanted to prolong my observation of him as a young man at a dinner party, not as his mother's distant, judging teenage son about to leave for college. He was enjoying himself, and that gave me great pleasure.

As dessert was being served, I went over to my son's table. He was in an expansive mood. Our friends at the table were leaning in to listen to him. I came up from behind, and heard them in conversation about the garden. I hung back quietly. None of them had seen the new garden, the new arrangement of trees, all the new plantings, the new paths, before that evening. And for all I could tell, my son had not seen them either. I was mistaken.

"The whole thing is changed," I overheard Alex saying. "Everything is different. Mom keeps making the beds bigger and bigger." He pointed to a spot in the back corner that had three evergreens planted in it. Everyone turned. "Look. That's where my swing set used to be. Gone, covered up by trees." Then he pointed to where his sandbox had been, a small wooden structure built and painted one afternoon by my father. "The sandbox is now covered with bushes," Alex explained. "The older we get, the more stuff disappears. The garden gets deeper and deeper. She is covering up our childhood."

I was stunned by my son. He did not sound angry at all. He sounded wistful, and a little perplexed. He sounded like *me*. For all his galumphing about leaving home and heading off to college that fall—in six months, in four months, in three weeks; he was crowing with glee over the rapid and inexorable march through time—he seemed reluctant to be leaving behind his swing set and his sandbox. I wondered if he understood that the sight of them was too painful to me; the time of my sons' childhoods had gone by quickly enough for me to be surprised that they were already grown up, but slowly enough for their abandoned toys to rot and collapse.

"Doesn't the garden look beautiful?" Alex said to our guests.

Teenagers can break your heart. Only by accident will you find out what they know—and it turns you inside out. I wanted to tell him that I was making the new beds for him, and for his brother, to return to, and for me to enjoy when they had left me behind at home. That the deepening and the widening, the planting and the pruning, the digging up and the covering up—the gardening—would never stop, could never stop, so long as I was there. And that I was only tucking into each bed, for safekeeping, my memories of all the time together we had been blessed with, in that garden.

But I didn't say a word.

Late that night, when I went to bed, I left the doors open to the balcony. I woke near dawn to find fireflies pulsing through my bedroom, tangled in my hair, dragging their tiny lanterns across my pillow.

· The End ·

# AFTERWORD

*"The garden's not enclosed.
It encloses her. It helps her
hold her joy."*
—Marie Ponsot
"Autumn Clean-Up"

The winter after the garden went in was a hard one; it felt like the first real winter in at least a decade. The snow began to fall at Thanksgiving, we had a white Christmas, and the snow kept falling, freakishly, into April. But the garden came through. Across town, the laurel and forsythia and daffodils and crocuses and pears and sassafras and cherry are bursting forth in all their cheerful, garish splendor. I had planted hundreds of daffodils the previous autumn, and was rewarded with a spring that seemed to last forever, and filled every vase I had. Some women have shoe addictions. I buy bulbs.

Bob D'Ambrosio appeared with the promised double-flowering bloodroot nestled in the bottom of a yogurt container. He was tanned and healthy-looking; he and his fiancée had spent the winter on the west coast of Florida. The bloodroot was a coy beauty; all of two inches high, its long white petals ruffled in the breeze of the spring afternoon (the temperature hit eighty degrees two weeks after the last snowfall). We planted the bloodroot at the base of the oak, just as he had said we would, close by the tilting concrete bench so that I would always know where to look for it. Bob also came bearing a basket the size of my fist; he had made it, one winter day in Florida, weaving hundreds of tiny slash-pine needles together with threads of raffia. The basket had a jaunty, pointed cap, tipped with a tiny Australian pinecone. He turned the basket over to show me his signature florette, made of raffia that he had dyed green. "Every year it's a different color," he said. "This is a basket to keep your dreams in."

And so, thank you to Bob D'Ambrosio for taking such good care of garden and gardener. The Helpful Men began to show up, all on the same day; the suburban spring was launched. The roofers came to unclog the winter's debris from the gutters, and to admit that some of them were tilting in the wrong direction and that was why the living room ceiling might be looking waterlogged. Leonard Pouder arrived—full of excitement about plans to expand his nursery— to admire the buzzing bounty of spring bulbs. Gary DiSisto drove up to check on the condition of the driveway, which is mercifully showing signs of heaving itself into the rumpled sort of state I so admire. Even my sons, Alex and Theo, began to show promising signs of usefulness. I have learned the art of bribery. I am ever grateful to the Helpful Men.

Thanks as well to my agent, Amanda Urban, and editors Nan Graham and Sarah McGrath. Stephen Orr, Deborah Needleman, and Elisabeth Rietvelt were my first readers, and the ones who cheered me on down this book's path and yanked me back when I strayed. Elisabeth's careful research has been invaluable. Keith Bearden checked for factual accuracy; if anything is wrong it is because I troweled in a few more things behind his back. Artist Neil Gower arrived from England, sketchpad in hand, and spent a day in the garden casting his own sort of spell; his bird's-eye view of the garden is at the front of the book.

Thank you, Peter Buckley, for helping to unearth a few things. Lora Zarubin, who is almost always hungry, brought new meaning to the garden party. And I am, as always, grateful to the trellis of friendship provided by Bonni Benrubi, Caroline Cunningham Young, and Zoe Mandes Billman. I lean on their love, and dedicate this book to them.

Yesterday the True Love left another gift in the garden. This time anyone could see it was a sign. It was pounded into the ground, at the beginning (or the end, depending on the direction you took) of the path through the Back Forty, and its brass letters read THE LONG WAY. Indeed, the path is endless, as in any garden that springs from the heart.

# ABOUT THE AUTHOR

Dominique Browning has been the editor in chief of *House & Garden* since 1995. She was previously the editor of *Mirabella,* an assistant managing editor of *Newsweek,* and the executive editor of *Texas Monthly.* She is the author of *Around the House and in the Garden: A Memoir of Heartbreak, Healing, and Home Improvement.* She lives in New York with her two teenage sons.